"*Enchanted One* brings us the inspired and inspiring message of divine love embodied. What could be more encouraging news as the world falls apart and we have an opportunity to rebuild it with a vision of sacred love?"

—*Daphne Rose Kingma, Author*

"The call to open our hearts to the power of real love can be very confusing but here, in this delightful book, Sheila has created a most inspiring blend of personal, practical wisdom dovetailed with spiritual information from the highest of sources. I am sure that *Enchanted One* will help anyone looking for support or spiritual guidance as they navigate the complex and often stressful challenges of daily living."

—*Mano Mannaz: Spiritual Artist and Author,*
Glastonbury, England

"I am so grateful for this timely piece of literature. I have always know my calling was to teach but, I couldn't find the whole truth in anything that I tried. Reading *Enchanted One* so inspired me. It felt like a flood gate had opened and everything came back, I remembered, and it was wonderful. Everything I tried or read before insisted that in some way I needed to accept an external power/ force as the ultimate guide or influence needed to complete me. In this book I finally found a clear explanation to questions and ideas I have grappled with since I was a little girl. Messages from Isis and Mary resonate so with me that I am covered by goose bumps, tears of relief and understanding stream down my face, when I read them. Through reading this book I am seeing how everything fits together. I now see how, what seemed to be the 'separateness' of events and experiences, was always only the next logical step."

—*Jacqueline, Life Coach from South Africa*

"*Enchanted One*, is a beautiful experience and revelation into seeing and understanding our journey here on earth. In reading I discovered many wonderful messages, in re-reading I found amazing answers. The book its self is a gem all should experience, however Sheila's gifts and insight combined, set the lighting to brilliance."

—*Diane Shenandoah, Faith Keeper for the Oneida Nation*

"*Enchanted One* is profoundly inspiring -- A must read for any spiritual seeker. It is the most beautiful and the most luminous book of our time."

—*Cynthia Powers-Broccoli, New York*

"In *Enchanted One*, Sheila Applegate honors us by sharing lessons from her life, including channeled messages from Isis and Magdalene. Her life, which unfolds before our eyes, inspires us and becomes our journey. We walk with her as she shares love in all its forms and then we are reminded to embrace all of our emotions. While this book feels familiar, the invitation to live in unconditional love is compelling."

—*Liala Strotman, Seeker, Healer, Educator,*
Long Island, NY

"*Enchanted One* is that message in a bottle sent directly from Mary Magdalene, Isis and our Creator to help us remember we are all a part of that Great Ocean, no drop separate from the other. Sheila Applegate is gifted enough to be able to receive this message of love and generous enough to share it with us in these few pages."

—*Rochette Withers, New York*

"Sheila has been my teacher of the *Oneness* for many years. It's due to her teaching that my understanding and knowing of the Divine within myself grows deeper and deeper each year. In her new book , *Enchanted One*, Sheila sets out to enlighten each reader of the truth of divinity within everyone and everything, and she succeeds extraordinarily well. A must read for all seekers."

—*Melina Carnicelli, New York*

"The depth of what *Enchanted One* covers: Fear, Ego, Grief, Re-membering, Forgiveness, Passion, Emotions... are all an expression of Love. *Enchanted One* can be read over and over again each time opening up to something new. It is full of tools and resources which can be used right now and every day."

—*Jennifer Johnston Roy,*
Director of Celebrate Today's Children

"Through *Enchanted One*, Sheila Applegate brings forth her most amazing, loving and spiritual healing energy that enables us all to live our true spiritual and God given potential: Enabling us to bring out our greatest desires to live and be creative in life. Sheila gives us the tools to make it happen."

—*Dr Rob Kiltz MD, Founder of CNY Healing Arts Center*
and CNY Fertility Center

Enchanted One

....

The Portal to Love

Enchanted One

. . . .

The Portal to Love

SHEILA APPLEGATE

TURNING
STONE
PRESS

First published in 2012 by
Turning Stone Press, an imprint of
Red Wheel/Weiser, LLC
With offices at:
665 Third Street, Suite 400
San Francisco, CA 94107
www.redwheelweiser.com

ISBN (paperback): 978-1-61852-046-3

Cover design by Jim Warner

Printed in the United States of America
IBT
10 9 8 7 6 5 4 3 2 1

Dedicated with love to:

Thomas L. Jocko
Darrell (Daz) Brown
And of course, Justin & Sarah Applegate

Contents

Acknowledgments

I would like to express my deeply felt gratitude to each soul on Earth and in spirit who touched my heart during my journey to remembering Oneness.

With special thanks to:

Clare Mallory, whose gift of editing brought forth the beauty of this message;

Laura Ponticello, for her passion and dedication to bring this story to the world;

Dustin Orofino, for seeing the portal and capturing the cover photo;

Patty and Mike Orofino, for supporting and believing in me.

Enchanted One

Enchanted One ~ You . . . and every person on Earth who awakens and embraces teachings of unconditional love.

Enchanted One ~ Magdalene . . . honoring the divine feminine, the expression of love that was taken from our history when Magdalene was removed from the story of Jesus and the Goddess energy was suppressed in story after story.

Enchanted One ~ Isis . . . the reflection of the Omega that has guided us since the beginning of time and comes now to bring us home.

Enchanted One(ness) . . . the enchantment of remembering our Oneness with divine love, the one source of creation, All That Is, God.

Introduction

Our world is enchanted. It is filled with love, grace, compassion, and souls passionate about their journey of awakening. Our world is now transforming through profound love. People from around the globe are uniting in hope of all that is to come.

Do you see this perfection in the world around you?

The world we live in is not free from pain, but you have the ability to create a world free from struggle for yourself.

In each situation, in every minute of each day, you have a choice, and the choice is always the same: "Do I choose to live from a place of love or a place of fear?"

My answer is, and always has been, love, in every situation. *This* is how I have learned to create a beautiful world around me. And *this* is what I want to share with you.

By no means am I asking you to live in an illusion or a bubble. You are a practical, rational being. You face life head-on. The lessons in this book are about embracing, not escaping. When you embrace the full spectrum of your emotions, increasing your awareness and moving deep into your shadows, you allow yourself to live in the power of unconditional love. *This* is how *you* will create the beautiful world your heart desires.

Over the past centuries, the heart-centered teachings of the divine feminine have been buried—not lost, but simply hidden until we as a collective group of souls on Earth were ready to understand and embrace them. We are ready now.

Whether you are aware of this or not, you are ready *now*, which is why your heart led you here.

This is the perfect moment for you to open your heart and receive the profound message of love that you have been seeking for so long. You are about to embark on a journey of unconditional love—the journey of the open heart.

This book is an expression of love through the open heart of the divine feminine. It weaves together teachings from two most beautiful and loving Goddesses.

Mary Magdalene is a soul whose embrace will guide you to open your heart and learn to love unconditionally. I am honored to share her teachings with you.

Years ago, as I embarked on my own journey of opening my heart, my whole world was turned upside down by the lessons of love and the levels of truth that were unfolding within me. One day, as I lay resting on my living room couch, a beautiful image of Magdalene appeared in front of me. At that point, I had already opened to my guides in meditations, but I was not accustomed to spirits appearing before me physically, and so I definitely took notice.

In that moment, Mary Magdalene put her hand on my heart and filled me with the deepest unconditional love I had ever felt. She then spoke, saying, "It is okay, I will walk with you through these next few years. I will be beside you all the way. I was Jesus's beloved and I understand the path you are walking. These next few years will be a challenge, but we will walk through this together." I felt profoundly comforted by her love. I did not even stop to think about what she meant by the "challenges" that were ahead of me. The year just prior to that, I had overcome a near-death experience, lost my best friend to cancer, and began to change the form of my partnership with my husband. What more could lie ahead? Little did I know how closely my journey would mimic that of the beloved Magdalene, a journey of love that would go beyond life itself.

As the years went by, Magdalene's loving embrace helped me through many challenges, and as I learned, I taught others. I led guided meditations and shared the messages of love that Magdalene offered me. Then, one day Magdalene said, "I want you to expand your awareness to include my vibration so that I can speak to these people directly."

I had seen others work in this manner before—Abraham as brought through by Esther Hicks is a messenger I respect—but when I heard Esther's early messages from Abraham, the thought of having another voice speak through me was frightening.

Yet there I was, with my beloved sister and spiritual guide asking me to be the vessel for her to speak.

My answer was, "No way!"

But Magdalene just smiled, and as her love poured into my heart, I surrendered.

The messages that came through Magdalene were deeply profound, and the love that poured through her was pure grace. How could I let my vanity and fear keep me from sharing her love with the world? I couldn't. Thus I began my new level of service with my beloved sister, Mary Magdalene. The union of our souls, in bringing the message of love to the world, continues to bless each of us.

As I worked with Magdalene, she introduced me to the vibration of Isis, a being of light known as the "Goddess of a Thousand Names." Isis is the divine feminine, the Omega. She is the purest reflection of God's love in feminine form—pure unconditional love.

This book includes messages of Mary Magdalene and Isis. The messages are direct and unfiltered. My thoughts and insights are woven throughout the chapters to help you integrate their wisdom into your daily life. Whether you believe the messages are directly from Magdalene and Isis or not, their truth remains profound. You have within you an innate ability to see Truth. I ask you to open your heart to receive the wisdom and love contained in this book. As the words resonate with you, open your heart and let them in. Let the love and truth contained in these words transform your life as they have mine.

Let the process of transformation open your heart and soul to a beautiful connection with the divine and to a world of love and joy. My hope is that you walk hand in hand with unconditional love.

In grace,
Sheila Applegate

A Word from Magdalene and Isis

An Introductory Message from Magdalene: The Time of the Goddess

My brothers and sisters of light, my brothers and sisters of God, my brothers and sisters of the Creator of All That Is . . . I come to all of you now, for we are all one, and the stories that were once given to small groups of people must be brought together, woven into one, that we will all remember the truth . . . for each one of these groups has remembered and held within their heart a certain piece of the picture.

Many of you have lived through many lifetimes—or you have studied many lifetimes—and so you understand many of their different aspects, but now it is time to bring it all together as one. So as you read these words that I have for you, I want them to touch each of you in your own way . . . I wish for these words to be about union, not about separation, so I ask for you to identify in, not out. What I mean by this is I ask for you to look for the parts of my story that resonate with you, that you understand, and that you feel, and I ask for you to identify them with your own lives, and in that space to expand outward, perhaps to receive some of the meaning of those things that don't quite make sense to you right now. Open your hearts that you will receive more than what you already know, but only that which you are ready to hear at this moment . . . for each one of us has our own journey, our own space and time with which we must open ourselves, and it is correct for you to follow your own journey . . . I do not wish to push anyone beyond their understanding at this moment, but I do wish to expand each one of you beyond your understanding at this moment.

And so with an open heart I come to you . . . I come to you with the messages that I have held in my heart. Some will say that injustice was served when my story was hidden . . . I say to you that the God/Goddess That Knows All would not have allowed a mistake of such magnitude to occur. Yes, it is a shame that for so many years the story was learned in a one-dimensional way, without its fullness. But let us not look at this as a failure on any part of man or religion. Let us look at it as a time for us to expand out the energies and learn emotions and things that without time we cannot understand fully, for beyond this realm there is a realm where there is no time and no space.

In that space which is no space, it is difficult at times for one to understand the multifaceted dynamics of things. Before time existed, when we expanded ourselves from the Creator God All That Is, we opened ourselves to what is known as the world of emotions . . . but in that time before time we did not understand emotions, and so when we felt something and all of our power was expressed immediately, we were very frightened. At that level in our power, we could destroy in an instant, lifting trees with our bare hands. As we began to understand this emotional realm, we knew that we must invent time . . . we, with our Creator God, expanded our understanding of God. We expanded the God energy to take the form you now understand as Earth, and in this realm we created time. Time was a gift for us to explore emotions in a slow and linear way—some might say like a scientific exploration; we had to dissect the emotions in order to understand and then master them.

I explain this to you now in reference to all the time that has passed since I walked this Earth as Magdalene, in all that time in which you may feel and remember resentment, especially those of you who associate and identify with the Goddess vibration. But I would like to say: let's not place our anger on the men that went before you, or the male energy, or the religion, or the politics that suppressed these understandings, because the very fact that those events occurred tells us all that we were not ready for these understandings at the time. Some were ready, and we passed that information down to them to hold until the time was right, but I have held within my heart all these memories until this time.

So this is why I say to you it is with such great joy that I am here now, ready to explain these things to you—the other half of the story, so to speak. For all those seeking God, all those trying to return to the Kingdom of Heaven through the love of their beloved brother Yasu, they are honored for this journey, as are those who seek the Kingdom of God through other means in the various areas of the world. They are honored for their journeys. We cannot just blame the Christians, as you call them, those who tell the story of Yasu, for taking the Goddess out: You will look across the world at many stories and see the Goddess removed. And in some places that held the Goddess energy, the God energy was removed . . . in linear time . . . learning one aspect and then the other until both aspects are learned and the truth, the whole truth, can be integrated once again.

So now is the time of the Goddess throughout the world, and you will see me rising upward now to speak to you, or coming downward to speak to you, on Earth. You will see Isis, my beloved sister whom I honor so much, coming to speak. You will see many Goddess energies rising up throughout the cultures, reminding those who have forgotten how powerful the energy of the Goddess is, the feminine aspect . . . I give great love and honor for all that my beloved has done, for all those things you have honored him with, but it would be an injustice if we did not share with you, now that you are ready, the understanding that it is the union of the male and the female, the God and the Goddess within . . . it is the remembrance of the union which is beyond any name . . . it is the remembrance of the whole soul, the Alpha and the Omega within, no longer split but coming together, that allows the miracles to occur. It is this union among people, among souls, and on our Mother Earth that will allow the ascension to occur on this planet.

And so, it is time now for us to hear the side of the Goddess, so that we can integrate and become whole once again, for as my beloved said to you, "These things and *more* shall you do." Now is the time for the "more," for when the masses return to the remembrance of the union of the Alpha and Omega within them, miracles will abound. We will no longer need the dense vibrations of linear time, and you will see this shifting. We will no longer need the dense vibrations of war and tragedy because we will have taken from them all that was necessary to learn . . . and harmony will occur once again . . . and the Earth's vibration will rise upward so that all of those souls will learn to live at the vibration that my beloved Yasu held and more. We will learn to live at the vibration that Isis, Osiris, and Horus lived at. But we will be more than that now because we will have learned emotions, and we will have mastered the feelings of anger and pain and transformed them into power and passion, and it will be used for harmony and union. Destruction will no longer be a thought—or it will no longer be necessary in our learning—and we will open the star gates together.

It has already begun. Many of you are speaking of the time in the near future when the star gates will open, but I say to you: do not look with your physical eyes for this to occur. Do not look to the outside, and do not look to the other planets. This does not come from a spaceship. This does not come from you in your mind, learning a way to transport into another time. Yes, it will affect the energies of your world, and you will see evidence of this, but the way and the key to the star gate that is opening before you comes from the heart. No one shall enter that kingdom without entering through the heart, through the space of divine love . . . and so, as the star gate opens, you will see that the veil will no longer be necessary, that souls will travel between the realms, and that the illusion of separation, while you are on Earth, will not be necessary. You will not need to go through the whole process of separation and remembrance. You will come down to the Earth when it is good to come down to the Earth, when you choose, just like going to any other space. You will travel between the realms as you now travel in the world, but you will not use compartments: You will use your heart, and you will go places that no vessel other than the vessel of the divine loving heart can take you.

No matter how much you remember your union with God and how much you live in that place, walking the Earth gives you dust . . . gives you dust on your chakras, gives you dust on your energy fields, because the Earth is dust. The Earth now is a density, and it is of time. It is of the illusion of separateness, and that will play heavily on you. And those of you who agree to be servants of the God/Goddess energy will take that on for others too, so that when your work is done you will start to lift that for others. No matter how evolved you get in your understanding and how you have united with the God/Goddess energy and felt that union, you must continue to do it every day. You must continue to cleanse yourself, and living in divine partnership is the greatest way to do this, whatever form that partnership takes . . . reflecting upon each other the truth and coming together in love—physical, emotional, and spiritual love—to heal those spaces, to purify and cleanse each other each day.

This is the gift that we offer you. This is the gift that will allow you to remember that you truly are the sons and daughters of the God/Goddess energy. Not only that, but you *are* the God/Goddess energy walking on Earth and reflecting back. This is why divine union and divine love are so important on this journey, and this is why we wish to teach you about unconditional love. This is why divine partnership is so important. We are not saying it has to be romantic. It can be between a child and an adult in parenthood; it can be among siblings or friends. But to live in divine partnership on Earth, to open your heart to love . . . unconditional love that goes beyond the ego, goes beyond expectations, goes beyond limitations . . . this is the gift of miracles that God offers you, that the Creator offers you, that All That Is reminds you of . . .

—*Magdalene, as channeled through Sheila*

An Introductory Message from Isis:
Opening the Star Gate

My children of light and my children of darkness, I call you both. Do you question me in this? I say to you that I see the shadows that dance inside of you, and I see the light that glows from within you, and both are beautiful. Have you not looked upon the skies and the Earth on a day in which the shadows danced, when the clouds were present and the sun danced against the trees? Have you not felt the beauty of that depth and known that it was the shadows that created that depth? For you cannot create beauty on Earth without the full spectrum of light, you cannot create this beauty without shadows and light. The embrace of dark and light dancing together creates this beauty. You cannot create your life by ignoring who you are, for in this space of Knowing, you are a powerful being, and you are here to explore. The life that you desire to create in the physical world is a reflection of the full spectrum of light, the full spectrum of emotion. Therefore, embracing all of it allows you to create that which you desire.

I say to you now that you are moving to the ability to be the observer and the participant . . . in the same moment you can be One With All That Is and have the amazing gift of walking on Earth beyond time and space. Time and space no longer have to rule you—you can rule time and space. You can use this gift to your advantage. You can decide how long you need, you can manipulate that as you can manipulate any energy. You say to me, "Won't that create havoc in the universe?" I say to you, it is time for there to be havoc in the universe. It is time now to disrupt the flow of linear thought pattern. It is time now to move beyond that. Each one of you who realizes the ability to step out of time and space long enough to create and then draw that creation back into time and space, each one of you here who does that, who uses that, who offers that gift, becomes Creator On Earth, embracing Mother Earth with the Divinity of All That Is. This is what it has been about.

Time was never intended to go on in linear form forever. In fact, it was never linear. That was an illusion that we created to explore. I say to you, what is happening now is happening always, for all has happened in one moment beyond time . . . in one "moment," and yet it is infinity beyond that, for it is outside of the realm of time and space. Everything is happening at once. Even as you create something you do not desire, in that same moment you are creating what you do desire. You no longer have to wait if you do not choose to wait. If you choose to create a delay, you will create a delay. If you choose to believe that things will still happen slowly, then that is what you will create in your life. You have an option now. We have gifted you now. We have welcomed you back. We have honored you for your journey. We have encouraged you to continue to explore the Earth realm with excitement and joy as you embrace every emotion from the space of participant and at the same time of observer . . . knowing that you are One and that it is an illusion, that it is simply part of the bigger picture.

So you place your focus down on that moment, and at the same time you embrace the expansiveness. And in this place, you have the ability to manipulate the energies around you and create the heaven that you desire here on Earth. There is no limit to this. The limit has been lifted by you with us—*all one*. Now we say to you: enjoy . . . enjoy . . . enjoy . . . enjoy. And if you do not like the way things are headed, stop yourself. Recreate it in that moment. Every moment, you recreate yourself and you recreate the life around you. Your thoughts create reality in a way that they have never done before. They have always created the reality around you, but now they create it in an instant. As long as you stay in the Now, you will have everything you desire. The way to stay in the Now is to be aware and to be present, to remember that you are embraced by the Alpha and the Omega, that you are supported, that you are *divine*, and that you have within you the ability to create that which is divine and nothing else . . . because there is nothing else.

You cannot make a mistake because all is perfect. All is Creation. You can release that feeling of separateness, that feeling of being punished, that feeling that you messed up as the Gods and the Goddesses in the heavens and created this Chaos. That fear is inside of you ready to be released now, and as you release that illusion, you re-gain your power, you remember . . . you embrace *now*. That is why I speak to you of fear and emotions. That is why your core . . . core . . . core understanding must be the desire to embrace that Oneness, to release the illusion of separateness, to become once again that memory of All That Is, to expand yourself in your relationships and your love, to embrace that knowing that you *are* all powerful, that you are God on Earth. Then, in that knowing of Oneness, bring that back down to your awareness of Earth, to your relationships, to your emotions.

This is the key that we are asking you to look at now. We are not asking you to remember this and to release the illusion in order to live in the heavens. We are not asking you to step out of the illusion of Earth. We are asking you to remember *and* choose to live in the moment of linear time, to be a part of the evolution, to embrace the moments of emotion, to explore the humanness, the experience of the full spectrum of emotions here on Earth, to be a participant with others on Earth, to share your knowing, to be witness to your knowing as you create that which you desire . . . because when you stay here on Earth, with that knowing, you draw that energy into this space so that Earth and heaven no longer have to be perceived as separate . . . so that the people of the Earth, the universal mind, become aligned with the understanding of this truth. And one by one, thousands by thousands, people begin to live in this space, and as a whole human race on Earth we begin to create a beautiful retreat center within the center heart chakra of the Divinity, of All That Is . . . so that we can always put our attention back to *this* cell of creation that vibrates once again in harmony with All That Is . . . so that we have the option at any moment of placing our attention in the realm of the tactile, the touch, the taste, the love, the vibration of emotions, all of that . . . and so that in that space we can mold and create with perfection. And then, when we desire, we can step into the vastness of *One*, we can move between that without limitation.

This is the *star gate* that is being created now, that people are speaking of in 2012 . . . I tell you, *you* are creating it now. This is the end of the Earth as you know it *and* the beginning of the Earth as you desire it. Be part of that Creation, embrace that now. Accept your power. Release your attachment to victimization, self punishment, limitation, and all of those things that keep you from creating what you want, that tell you "you can't," that keep you from the responsibility of remembering your Oneness. For there is no greater service on Earth than to embrace this

Oneness. This Earth is a playground for you to explore emotions, and it can be playful. Nothing will harm you as you explore your emotions, because you are vibrating in the love of God, and in this space there is perfection. Remember this now, and sit in that awareness.

—*Isis, as channeled through Sheila*

Part I

Love and Illusion

≈ 1 ≈

Love

Enchanted One ~ I surrender myself now . . . completely expanding to be filled with the vibration of divine love. Open my heart and my understanding that I may be free to embrace the joy and passion of living in unconditional love on Earth.

∼

Loving Unconditionally

As humans, we all want to be loved. This is really our ultimate quest here on Earth: to explore love, to learn to embrace the giving and receiving of this sacred energy. It seems like such a simple quest, and yet we work so hard to achieve it. Why?

We are actually born knowing how to love completely and unconditionally. We spend the next several years forgetting, as we are trained in a life of conditional love. Hopefully, if we are one of the lucky ones, we come to a point at which we wake up and once again begin the quest back to the innocence and truth of our ability to love beyond form, beyond condition.

From early childhood, we are programmed to doubt, fear, resist, and ask, "What's in it for me?" When I was a child and my mother wanted me to do something—clean the living room, for example—I would ask, "What will you give me for it?" She would say, "A kiss," in an almost teasing way. She was trying to point out that I should help because I loved her and we were a family, and yet at the same time she offered me a reward, and not even one I wanted. The energy of that offer was conditional love. "You do this for me, and I will give you love." In this case, it was a playful game that she played with us, and yet in life we are bombarded by many subtle messages that teach us to love conditionally. In our society, love is about meeting each other's needs; if we don't meet each other's needs, then we must not really love each other.

But what if we, as individuals, learn to meet our own needs? What if we learn how to become full and complete beings who are filled with the love of God, Creator, All That Is? What if we reach a point at which we don't *need* people to fill our needs, but rather all we *want* people for is to share this beautiful experience with us? What if we reach that point where we can embrace the full spectrum of emotions . . . yes, even anger, fear, and pain . . . while remaining in the bliss of love? *It is possible.* Look at an infant and remember.

The other day, I opened a fortune cookie and read it out loud. It said, "Everything ends." My son instantly responded with, "That's not true—*love* never ends!" From a child's lips, so trusting, so simple, so true. What if we really believe that? What will our lives be like when we believe that love never ends? We will be safe to love and, in that space, to be filled with joy. *Love never ends.* The whole rest of the morning, I was singing in my head a variation of a nursery school song: "This is the love that never ends . . . it just goes on and on, my friend . . . some people started feeling it not knowing what it was . . . and they'll continue feeling it forever just because . . . this is the love that never ends . . . it just goes on and on, my friend . . . some people . . ."

Love is simple. Living in unconditional love is our natural state, so why do we work so hard at it? Last night, I was running a meditation. Two little girls were in the group. I explained to them that we were going to hear a story and that our imaginations would lead us on a beautiful journey. I also explained that, because there were a lot of grown-ups in the room who had forgotten how to imagine, we would have to take our time and explain things to them because they were working very hard to get back to the place where children are naturally. One of the little girls looked into my eyes, and I knew she understood. In that moment, I asked her if she would make me a promise to use her imagination as she grew up so that she would not have to come back later and relearn how to do what she already knew now. She looked me deep in the eyes and made a promise that I know she will remember. I could feel it all through her, and different points in her life flashed before me, points in her future when that simple moment would return to her and she would remember.

Remember. That is how Mary of Magdalene asks us to look at it. When we are learning, searching, clearing, healing, seeking . . . we are simply in the act of *remembering*, returning to the awareness that we are One with All That Is, part of the ever-moving flow of pure, sacred, unconditional love. Everything else is an illusion. If you are a parent, a grandparent, a teacher, an aunt, an uncle, or a neighbor of a child, make it your vow to create the space for the children of today to live in this Truth. Teach them love instead of fear, and this world will become an oasis of peace. It is that simple.

It *is* that simple. We are love. God is love. Everything that exists is love, and that is *all there is*. There is nothing more than that. If you believe this to be true but have not been able to fully embrace it or live from this place in every moment of your life, then keep reading, and hopefully something I say will help move you to that centered space where your heart and mind are one in this Truth. If you *want* to believe it, you are halfway there! These teachings and their momentum will carry you home . . . home to your birthright and to the never-ending flow of divine love.

Loving Myself

> *"If you look up into the sky and think, 'I am just a tiny piece of this huge universe,' remember that a puzzle is useless without all its pieces."*
>
> —Sarah Applegate

The best place to start loving is the one place most of us avoid at all costs. Love yourself! Fall in love with yourself! Have a love affair with yourself!

Look in the mirror. Right now. Put this book down and go look in the mirror. Look at yourself for five minutes, and then come back and read the next paragraph. If you read ahead, you will never be able to get this moment back because you will know what I am going to say, so take the time, the risk, and the energy to give this a try before reading on.

Now that you've taken the time and looked in the mirror for five minutes, ask yourself the following questions about your experience: How comfortable was I looking at myself? Which did I notice first—the things I like about myself, or the things I think of as my flaws? Could I even see my beauty? Could I see things that I perceived as flaws?

How you perceived yourself in the mirror will give you an idea of how well you are able to love yourself as a reflection of God on Earth. But it is also more than that. *How* you looked at yourself has everything to do with how you conduct yourself in your relationships. All of our relationships are mirrors of our own personal truth, and so if we believe we are beautiful and love ourselves, we will see that same love reflected back to us in the people who are in our lives. If we look for the beauty in ourselves first, we will look for—and find—the beauty in others and in our situations. If we are looking for our flaws, chances are we will find them in others.

Loving ourselves is not a concept that we are taught to embrace. How many times have you seen this scenario in one form or another: Someone tells a young child, "You are so beautiful/smart/loving/strong." The child answers, "I know," and the adult suddenly turns red-cheeked and giggles nervously, telling the child, "You shouldn't say that," or, "Don't be vain." We are taught from such a young age that to claim our strengths is vain. In a sense, we are taught to be ashamed of knowing how wonderful we are. But if we truly believe we are a reflection of God's love on Earth, we should be shouting it from the rooftops! We knew this truth as children, and we can get back there as adults.

The first step in the path back to our truth is to notice the dust that has piled up on us during these years of living in our illusion. We have to open our eyes to the awareness of how much of that illusion we have bought into simply by being human. We begin with self exploration and awareness. Start to open your eyes and ask yourself, "Who are you?" "What do you like?" "What do you believe?" "Why do you believe these things?" So many times, we take on belief systems without even realizing that we have done so. No one *intends* to reduce children with limiting belief systems; we simply pass on what we "know." But if we don't take the time to really consider what we "know," then we are simply passing down old belief systems without allowing them to change. The best gift we can give ourselves is the gift of exploring our truth. Life is about change, and if we hold on to a belief system that is outdated, we are not allowing ourselves to be in the flow of life.

Parents have labeled the developmental stages of two- and three-year-olds "the terrible twos" and "the trying threes." Those labels contain within them a powerful belief system that has been passed down from generation to generation without even a second thought. Two-year-olds are known to test; they are exploring their world and testing their limits. They question authority and express their full spectrum of emotions with passion. And we call that the "terrible twos." Three-year-olds question everything. "Why?" comes out of their mouths so often that even the most aware mother resorts to "just because!" out of pure exhaustion. And so we call that the "trying threes." It's ironic that we've labeled such an early stage of development as something negative, because that's the exact stage we need to go back to in order to reclaim our truth—to become "as little children."

The first step in our self-awareness is to question everything; don't take *anything* for granted. Don't assume that any of your beliefs are set in stone. It can be exhausting and even a bit unnerving in the beginning, just as it is with the "trying threes," but you will soon find that you are falling in love with yourself as you wipe away the dust and see once again the shining gem beneath the surface.

Self-awareness on this level is only the first step. This self-awareness is the awareness of yourself as a human being. You are stripping away the layers of dust and tarnish that you were not even aware had built up on your psyche. Once you start to see the treasure that is beneath the surface, you remember that you are a piece of God's divine creation. Now is the time to reconnect with that truth.

As you begin to follow your path to Oneness, you seek out your higher power by whatever name resonates with you. There is only one Creator God, and this is divine love. There are many paths to the truth and many ways of describing it on Earth, so follow that which resonates with you. All is God, and therefore no matter which path you take, which language you use, which story you resonate with, you will find the truth. If you are seeking love, you will find love. Even if you are not seeking love, you will find love because love is All There Is.

For me, the journey to this awareness consisted of many different techniques and stories. It was important to me from a very young age to incorporate many different religions: I understood God on a personal level, and I knew that the loving God who filled my life would not exclude anyone seeking that love. And so, from a young age, I sought out the truth in every religion that I came across. I found that in each religion I explored there was love, which to me is a reflection of God, and there was fear, which is a reflection of the human illusion of separateness. I made love my quest. I discovered that guided meditations helped me reconnect directly with the beings of light that reflect love. I learned to reconnect to my *I am* presence, or higher self, expanding my vibration, clearing the dust of my humanness, and remembering my Oneness. Through prayer, meditation, surrender, and partnership, I cleared the dust of illusion from my surface and became once again a mirror of divine love, a pure refection of God's love in human form.

And as I remembered the God in me, it was easier for me to see the God in others. I began to look through the dust and see God's light in all people. In this state, I fell in love with God's love, in love with myself, in love with others, in love with life itself. In this state, I began to realize that everything I had experienced since the beginning of time had been perfect.

The following is a journal entry that captures a moment in my journey when I fell in love with love itself.

I Fell Head Over Heels in Love Again

It started on Wednesday at the beach, and then on Thursday morning we took a dolphin watch boat ride . . . and that is when it overtook me. I was standing on the bow of the boat, sea wind in my hair, the taste of salt on my lips, the sky filled with the bright sun and puffy white clouds, the shoreline of Victorian homes and hotels on the horizon . . . and suddenly I was overtaken.

It started with butterflies in my tummy and rose to a complete explosion in my heart, as I fell head over heels in love with God again . . . the love was so huge it overtook me. I did not care what games He may have played with my heart . . . I knew they were all for my own good. I don't care if He breaks my heart a thousand times . . . I will jump through hoops for Him to have this feeling, this complete Oneness with all of creation, the sense of not knowing where my hand ends and His begins, the complete awe of His creation and, yes, His divine and beautiful plan. I was exploding with such unconditional love, I knew all of creation could hear me, and I could hear all of creation . . .

Then I called out to the dolphins . . . everyone was waiting to see them . . . and I sent out a vibration from my heart, and I felt them respond. I knew in my heart they were coming, and within a minute three separate pods of dolphins came swimming in, jumping and dancing in the water all around us, coming so close to the boat we could see the droplets of water on their skin . . . and my heart burst with even greater adoration for my Creator. There was nothing in the world that mattered more than His love for me . . . and this I know. I am so completely in love with God that nothing else matters. I will face whatever is placed in front of me because His love and His divine plan are so grand that I am in awe of His glory, His intricate and delicate plan to bring me *all* of my heart's desires . . .

Everything I face on Earth is perfection, and I want for nothing . . . this is my only truth.

2

True Forgiveness

Enchanted One ~ I open my heart and expand my understanding now that I may remember that everything that has ever happened in my life and in my relationships has been in perfect harmony with my journey of awakening. I am a perfect expression of divine love on Earth. I embrace myself and all those around me with unconditional love and gratitude for all that has been given for me.

~

A Message from Magdalene on the Subject of Forgiveness

You are One with the Creator. You are not separate, you are not alone, you are not weak, you have not been misguided or left behind from God, All That Is, the Creator. You are whole. You do not need to seek outside of yourself to become whole, you are a (w)holiness within yourself. You do not have to redeem yourself; you only need to remember that union. When you open up to this divine love, what are the fears that arise? No longer of your weaknesses, for I say to you, every one of you who has walked this Earth for so many lifetimes, or so many years (whichever you wish to think), you have mastered weakness.

You have become masters of fear and weakness. You have been masters of bending down on your knees and separating God, and asking Him—Him—to come save you. When you open to the truth of love, you feel the power of the God/Goddess energy entering you as you recall your union . . . as you remember that you never separated from your Beloved, that your souls have always been One, that inside of *you* is the Alpha and Omega, that you are a reflection of God in wholeness. Everything else that you make yourself to be, in separation from God, *that* is sin . . .

Separate . . . Illusions . . . Now . . . SIN . . . Separate . . . Illusions . . . Now . . .

You have spoken of sin for so many years, and you have put moral obligations around this. You have set structures of words . . . "This will make you sinful," and "This will make you of God," and "You are sinful but God will come and redeem you." Yes, as long as you are separate in your illusions now, in that moment there is sin. In the moment that you believe in the separation of your union with the God/Goddess energy, that is sin. Whatever you do or say in that moment is sin. It doesn't matter if you are speaking wonderful truths; if you are speaking them from this space, you are separate from that remembrance.

What is forgiveness? Forgiveness is the moment that the God/Goddess energy pours into you and you remember once again that everything that occurs here on Earth and in the Heavens is given for you . . . Given For . . . For-Given. It is necessary, it is given for you out of necessity for you to learn.

Let me repeat what I have said to you now, what sin and forgiveness are. Sin is when you are separate in your remembrance and your illusion, being in the illusion now of separateness. Being in the illusion now of separateness is the only sin that can occur. Remembrance is forgiveness because in the space of remembrance you recall that everything that is done, that has been done, and that you have done has been given for you in order to help you remember your union with God, the Creator of All That Is.

I say once again, many of you have been very comfortable with living in the separateness, living in the fear and not taking responsibility here on Earth, looking to God to save you rather than remembering inside of yourself that you are the God/Goddess that saves you. There is, yes, a beloved energy that looks over you, but it is a part of you. It looks at you in the same way that you would look at a small child held in your arms. If you hold an infant to your heart, you feel that Oneness and yet you cannot see it, so you pull that child away from you and look into its eyes, and you feel that love even more. That is the expansion that has occurred between you and God. You have pulled yourself away from God, so that you can look into the eyes of God and God can look into the eyes of you and you can remember through that love that you are One. You are filled with the Separation of Illusion Now, and so you think perhaps that you are unworthy of that love. Until you remember . . .

—Magdalene, *as channeled through Sheila*

∼

Opening to love inevitably brings us to a very powerful understanding of forgiveness. When we truly reach the place of surrendering into divine love, we begin to understand that *everything that has ever occurred* has been perfect. *We are not victims. No one has ever wronged us.* This is hard for us to take in. True forgiveness is *not* accepting that someone has wronged us and deciding to forget it and move on. True forgiveness is coming to the understanding that everything you have ever faced in life has been a gift of love to bring you closer to your remembrance of Oneness with the Creator. Yes, even the most painful lessons are gifts of love.

You truly will not be capable of loving another soul unconditionally until you have learned to love and forgive yourself. Magdalene says forgiveness is "given for us." When we can reach a point where we truly believe that *all* situations, *everything* in our life, *anything* anyone has ever done "to us" is perfect and "given for us" to help us learn unconditional love, then we are truly experiencing forgiveness. It is very different from saying, "This person harmed me, but I will forgive them." No—to practice true forgiveness is to say, "Thank you for creating the space in which I could learn more about myself, remember my union with God, and embrace love more fully."

How do we get to the point where we can do this? *We love ourselves!* If we truly love ourselves in this moment, then we *can* be grateful for everything that has ever happened to us because those things are what have helped form who we are in this moment. If we do not love ourselves, we won't be able to see this perfection, and as a result we will guard ourselves. When we guard ourselves, we aren't able to love with an open heart: We protect ourselves from all those "scary" people and situations that can hurt us like we've been hurt before, we define ourselves and our relationships by our past, and we are incapable of showing up in the present.

We need help getting back to that space of being able to love and embrace ourselves in order to love and receive love in its purest form. This is the journey of our awakening. It is our quest to God, and it can come in many forms. One of the stories of this quest that is most dear to my heart is that of the Haudenosaunee (Iroquois) Peacemaker. As with most stories of prophets and transformation in history, there are many versions of the Peacemaker's Journey. The following is a glimpse of my understanding as it relates to the teachings of forgiveness.

Haudenosaunee (Iroquois) legend tells of The Great Peacemaker who came in a stone canoe from across the lake to bring the message of peace to warring tribes of the east. The Peacemaker came to the home of a powerful warrior whom we know now as Hiawatha. The Peacemaker climbed to the roof of Hiawatha's home and lay down by the smokehole. As Hiawatha looked into the pot that was cooking his meal, he saw the reflection of the Peacemaker in the broth. He thought that it was his own reflection. Seeing the peace in the face reflected in the water, Hiawatha was transformed. His heart opened. As he saw himself in a new light, he looked into the eyes of the Peacemaker's reflection and saw his own potential.

Hiawatha began to live in peace and sought to teach others of this way. As happens in times of war, there was much fear among the people of the land, and it was difficult for him to get others to follow the way of peace. It is said that as Hiawatha spoke up of the message of peace, the Tadadaho, an "evil sorcerer," retaliated, using his powers to kill Hiawatha's family.

Hiawatha wandered the land for months, grieving the loss of his daughters. While grieving at Song Lake, he took notice of the beautiful purple and white shells known as Wampum. As the birds flew from the water, his grief lifted with them, and he realized he needed to forgive in order to find peace in his heart. Collecting the beautiful purple and white shells, Hiawatha strung them on a piece of sinew. As he ascended the mountain, the Peacemaker came to him and spoke of each shell and the process of healing. As the Peacemaker sang a song of grief, he wiped Hiawatha's eyes so he could see clearly again, his ears so he could hear the Creator once more, his throat so he could breathe without grief, and his heart to allow him to love again. As Hiawatha's love returned, he descended the mountain with the Peacemaker, and, together with Jikonsahseh Mother of the Nations, they walked down the mountain and traveled through the water to the swamp where the Tadadaho lived. Together they sang the song of love as they approached the Tadadaho, and it was through this loving forgiveness that the Tadadaho opened his heart. Once his heart was opened, the Peacemaker told the Tadadaho that he would continue to lead the people but that he would do it with love, not fear. The Tadadaho agreed to follow the way of the Peacemaker and to guide the Haudenosaunee people in doing the same.

This is a story of profound forgiveness and transformation. In order for Hiawatha to continue on his own personal journey of peace, and to witness this to others, he had to accept that even the death of his family was to be embraced with love. A similar expression of forgiveness is found in the teachings of Jesus, when, on the cross and faced with death, He said, "Father, forgive them, for they know not what they do."

I, too, was faced with a similar situation in my own life, when I had to decide whether or not to forgive the people in the car that had hit and killed my beloved. Today, as I write this, it is the third anniversary of the day my beloved twin flame crossed to the spirit world, killed by a car in a hit-and-run accident. A few days after he died, the children who had been in the car that had hit him turned themselves in. They were from the same small community, and I had known two of them since they had been small children. I can honestly say that I never felt that I could not forgive those teens. How could I, when I had known my beloved's death was coming? Weeks before his death, we had witnessed his ascension, and with the help of the spirit world we had prepared for it. I had not known exactly how or when it would occur; on Earth, it was an accident, a series of "bad choices." But beyond that, it was the unfolding of a divine plan that would allow my beloved twin flame to serve the Creator in an even greater way than he could have on Earth. It would allow him to walk with me beyond any illusion of separation and expand his love and service to levels I could not even conceive of at the time. So how could I condemn the people or the choices that had created this circumstance? I could not. I felt only compassion for those teens. That did not exclude me from experiencing the full spectrum of emotions that come with grief; I have cycled through all of the emotions, even anger, over the three years since his death. And yet I know beyond a doubt that all that has occurred has been perfect and therefore was "given for me."

This is the forgiveness I ask you to seek in your own life—not for me, but for your own peace. For it is in this space that you will truly remember that you are God's love on Earth. In this space, you will be free to live with an open heart to experience the full spectrum of emotions with passion, to walk in divine partnership with others. When you truly believe that you are embraced by the divine, you will not feel the need to protect yourself from emotions evoked by the world. And in this space, you will be free to live in love's embrace.

~ 3 ~

Remembering Our Wholeness

*Enchanted One ~ I rest in the vibration of divine love as
I open my heart and expand myself into the awareness of
All That Is. I am a Whole and Beautiful hologram of the
universe breathing love on Earth.*

~

Remember, *remember*, we are *one* with God, the Creator of All That Is. As we journey to this remembrance, we must often follow a path of exploration. We
use various techniques such as those I have spoken of to
"heal" our misconceptions. We explore the thought patterns and behaviors that no longer serve us and seek to
release them.

I have seen many people on the path to awakening
get caught in the process of healing. We work so hard to
heal and learn in order to remember that we are One with
God, that the process of awakening itself can become a
habit that keeps us from living in our truth. We have to
be careful not to fall in love with the process itself. Spiri-
tuality can become so satisfying that we lose sight of the

reason we're on the path to begin with: to return to our truth as divine love, to love unconditionally from a place of loving ourselves.

Our goal is to simply remember that we are perfect now. We are each a reflection of God's love on Earth. We simply are. Everything we do and say is a reflection of that love. If God and divine love truly are all that is, then nothing can be separate from that. We do not have to work our way back to that, we do not have to clear and heal ourselves so we will become worthy of being One with God: We already *are* One with God . . . we have simply forgotten. So our quest here is not to *become* pure love, it is simply to remember that we already *are* pure love.

The journey is personal, and yet, whether we realize it or not, we are all seeking the same thing. How we do that can vary; each of us has our own way of returning to our true self. Concerning ourselves with how others do it simply means we are avoiding our own work. We can certainly learn from each other's experiences, but ultimately we are each here to find our own way back to our divinity.

When I was about twelve years old, I attended a weekend retreat for the Protestants in my area. During one of the worship services, they asked us to raise our hands if we had not asked Jesus Christ to be our personal savior. I had never actually heard about accepting Jesus as my personal savior, and I didn't know what it meant. Jesus was my friend and my teacher. He was a part of my daily life. But I didn't know what it meant for him to be my savior. I didn't even know I had to be saved. What did I need to be saved from, anyway? Fear came over me. How could I have missed such an important part of life with Jesus? What was going to happen to me if I didn't do this? So I raised my hand, and they took us into a back room. I remember the musty smell of the camp bunk and the Bible they made me read from. I don't know what was said, but I do remember that I had to say specific words that would save me from hell. Phew! Good thing I hadn't missed that one! I remember leaving with a mix of relief and confusion. And yet I didn't feel different . . . except maybe more confused. Jesus had already been a part of my life, and saying these words had not changed that in any way.

Language, although beautiful in helping us relate to each other as humans, has the power to both unite and divide. The above story illustrates this. The language used by the workshop leaders was merely a restatement of what I had already known in a different context. Our attachment to the language we use and the stories we tell has led to centuries of misunderstanding, separation, and fear. Now, thirty years after my camp experience, when I come across new language for what I already know, I remind myself that I am One . . . I remember I am One . . . I am perfect Now. In each situation that presents itself to me, I look for that gem of insight or energy that helps me on my journey without going back and trying to do the same work over and over again. I am here to love. I am here to love myself.

All is love. There is nothing else.

Loving ourselves unconditionally is simple. Babies do it. Puppies do it. We as humans, however, are not simple. I have worked very hard to return to my truth. I am driven to explore every emotion, to face and embrace every situation with passion, to embrace the lessons given to me, but it took me a long time to reach this point.

When I was a teenager, I was told repeatedly that I was "dramatic" and "too emotional," and I started to believe it. But being emotional was not always pleasant, and so I sought out and found a partner who would "balance" me. I basked in his "neutral" energy. I was a bird soaring through the sky, and his energy was like a tree I could rest in. On the surface, I felt "complete," but in the process I had tried to shut out my emotions, or at least to control them, and this did not work for me. Passion called to me, and I had to feel again. When I finally started my journey to embrace my emotions once again, it was like going through hell for a while. I had stuffed so many emotions down during those years since teenhood that now I had to purge them.

Emotions don't just go away. They remain inside of us waiting to be released, and when something triggers us they come up like a flood. That scares us, and so we shut them back down again. The problem is that shutting down to one emotion is impossible without shutting them all out. When we refuse to feel our fears, pains, or anger, we block ourselves from feeling love. In that moment that we shut our heart to protect ourselves from feeling whatever emotion we are afraid of, we have shut off the flow of love . . . or, to be more accurate, we have shut out our *remembrance* of that flow . . . our remembrance of Oneness. Love is always there, always flowing, always available. We are simply afraid to let it in. Why would we be afraid of love? Because to let love in, we have to open our hearts, and if we open our hearts, we will have to experience *all* of the emotions we refused to experience the first time around. This is what keeps us from moving forward.

Buried emotions will surface. Someone may say something and we explode with emotion, only to wonder later why we reacted so strongly to something so innocent. If we go on suppressing our emotions, we will find them bursting out of us like steam from a pressure cooker. I have seen so many people start on the path of opening their heart only to get to the center of their emotions and turn back because it seems too hard . . . only to try again later . . . and again later.

All attempts on the path to discovering our emotions are perfect because any action we take toward living with an open heart will help bring us closer to our experience of our Oneness. I see purging emotions like a wall of fire that we have to move through in order to reach the side of passionate peace we are seeking. We want it so much that we walk toward it, and then, often, right when we get in the middle of the purging, the flames seem so intense that we turn back . . . only to have to walk through that same wall of fire again later. But if we stop to realize that when we are in the center of the wall of fire it is equally as difficult to walk back to where we came from as it is to go forward to the other side, we would choose to keep going, to reach the other side, where we would never have to purge those emotions again!

After purging our emotions, crossing the fire, we still continue to feel the full spectrum of emotions—anger, fear, and pain are still a part of life—but when we have cleared the past and stand in the present with an open heart, those emotions are felt in a way that is simply related to the present, to a specific incident. We no longer open a floodgate of emotions that have been waiting to be released for a lifetime. Just like a small child, we cry, scream, shake . . . and then it is gone . . . and peace and love flood back to the empty space, and we continue on. It is that simple.

The most important thing to remember on this path is that you do not have to do this alone. As soon as you are ready to live with an open heart, the universe, God, the Creator, the vibration of divine love will pour into you and assist you on this journey. For me, this has included guided meditations in which I have learned to work closely with my own spirit guides. Sitting in the space of peace and allowing the energy of love, spirit guides, and ascended masters help you to transmute the ideas, beliefs, and concepts that no longer serve you will carry you further than you can believe. It is not meant to be difficult. Everything is aligned to assist you on this journey. Open up and let the help in.

~ 4 ~

Loving the Ego

*Enchanted One ~ I embrace my ego with love and under-
standing. I give gratitude for the role that this gift of ego
awareness has played in my awakening. Together, we move
forward as One in perfect union of mind, heart, and spirit.*

~

As a Spiritual Life Coach, I help people integrate
spiritual understanding and Oneness into their
daily lives. One of my clients entered my office and
immediately started talking about the struggle she had
been having with her ego flaring up on her over the past
few weeks. I gave her a mini version of my philosophy
about the current ego movement. She said she was, in
fact, reading the book *A New Earth*. She went on to say
that she had "corked" her ego so she could show up clear
for the reading. I told her, "Oh no! You can't *fight* it—you
have to *love* it!" Her jaw dropped and her eyes bulged.
She looked at me as if my words were blasphemy . . . as if I

were asking her to worship the devil. No, I was not saying she should worship her ego, just that she should love it! It was then that I realized I was being called to talk more about loving the ego . . .

Once again, my friends, *everything is God!* Separation is an illusion. The ego, the little "I," is a natural result of our expanding consciousness that allows us to experience the Earth's gifts. These gifts include touch, taste, smell, emotions, and even sex. The Earth experience is an adventure in which the God that is All That Is expanded in order to explore the canvas of emotions and senses. As a result of this expansion and the experience of emotion, humans began to feel separate from God. The part of God that we are as souls began to believe that we were separate . . . we began to fear for our survival, and the ego formed to protect us. Anger was the ego's job, a response to the emotions of fear because, in the days of survival, fear indicated a threat to our lives. And so the little ego of ours did well by us.

But now we are here, having explored the world of Earth and all of its senses and emotions, and we are waking up and remembering that we are One with God, that we were never separate, and yet we feel the need to fight against the very part of us that led us to this point as a human race. Once again, that is an illusion. If the ego is something to fight against or overcome, then it is not of God, and that is impossible because God is All There Is. Once again, God is All There Is, and so the ego, too, is of God.

What happens when we recognize that even the ego . . . even the Universal ego . . . is God? We pour love into this part of God, and as we remember *we* are God, the ego expands into our highest self and we ascend to become masters on Earth . . . And in this space, anger becomes passion, fear becomes excitement, guilt becomes surrender, greed becomes service, sex becomes creation . . . and we are whole again, as we have always been. In this place, we begin to experience the bliss of being spirit on Earth . . . we become the sight, scent, voice, taste, and touch of God, and we offer back to All That Is the complete ecstasy of loving God's creation with completeness.

Transforming our ego from the primitive survival instinct with which it was originally programmed into a supportive guide on our journey to remembering our Enchanted Oneness is essential to our awakening process. Spirit loves to play with the words we use in order to give us new understanding. Last night I asked spirit, "What I should call the evolved ego?" And with a big grin my beloved answered, "WeGo." I love this thought because we are indeed expanding our individualized perception of survival to the Universal One in movement: WeGo.

I have been given a daily visualization exercise to help transform the primitive ego to the supportive WeGo. Taking a moment each morning and throughout the day to sit in this visualization will accelerate your awakening process and bring effortless grace to your day.

WeGo Meditation

Sit comfortably with your back straight. Take a deep breath in and release. Continue to breathe deeply and rhythmically as you feel your body becoming more and more relaxed. All distracting thoughts float away like puffy white clouds in a deep blue sky; they have no power over you. As you sit, relaxed and comfortable, you begin to see, feel, or sense above your head the beautiful golden sun. Beyond this sun is another golden light of the central sun, The God Center, All That Is. As you draw your attention to the central sun you begin to see the golden light of the central sun pouring downward to fill the physical sun. This light continues to pour downward until it reaches just above your head: your crown chakra. The golden light then fills your crown chakra, entering into your head bringing into harmony now every cell of your physical, emotional, and spiritual bodies. The light continues downward . . . filling your eyes that you see only the truth, filling your ears that you hear only the truth . . . filling your throat that you speak only the truth and that you speak this truth with grace and strength. The light continues to move through every cell of your physical, emotional, and spiritual bodies, bringing all of you into complete harmony. Allow this light to enter your heart . . . filling every chamber of your heart . . . opening you to give and receive love in its fullness. The golden light continues to move downward to just below your ribcage, your solar plexus . . . the emotional center of your body. Allow the golden light to bring into harmony now *all* of your emotions, so that you will be free to experience the full spectrum of emotions with love and grace. Then feel that golden light continue downward into your midsection, the Creation Center of your body. Allow the light to flood your Creation Center, cleansing and preparing the space now to become the womb of all your desires. Then feel that golden light pour out of your tailbone and onto Mother Earth . . . wrapping around and filling your legs as it pours through your tailbone and into the Earth.

Like golden rings of water rippling out, the golden light fills the entire surface of Mother Earth and then penetrates into the Earth's center. The golden light pours all the way into the center of Mother Earth, the Fire Core, the God Center of our Earth. You are now completely connected to heaven and Earth. Sit for a moment in this vibration. Then feel the golden light of Mother Earth's Fire Core expanding outward to fill all of the Earth. When the golden light of Mother Earth reaches you, it begins to fill you, pouring through your tailbone and into your Creation Center. Then the golden light continues to move upward into your Heart Center, where this vibration of golden light expands outward. You are now sitting in complete Oneness as the golden light pours through you in all directions. Rest in this space for as long as you like. When you are ready, draw your attention back into the center of your body where you feel energy of One forming a rod of light running parallel to your spine, connecting both to the central sun through your crown chakra and to the Fire Core of Mother Earth through your tailbone. In this space you feel completely aligned with Enchanted One and present in your own body. Take a deep breath. Open your eyes. Smile and enjoy your day.

The Illusion of Addiction

"You have been battling the entity of addiction since the beginning of time, and it has always been an illusion."

This is the message that my cellular body shared with me during a session of Neuro-Emotional Technique (NET) a few years ago. The moment I received that message, I felt a sense of knowing and release. However, today, two years later, I hear the same quote repeating itself in my head. Today, I have come to a deeper understanding of what this means to all of us.

Across the nation, people are opening their eyes to a new understanding. Oprah has brought people together to explore the ego through Eckhart Tolle's book, *A New Earth*. People who have never considered these concepts are opening up to them and exploring the ego is becoming a conversation across the country. Those who have been on a journey of self-exploration are finding new words and understanding for their struggle. Even people who have not laid a finger on the book are being affected by this movement. I have noticed in my personal life as well as in my role as a spiritual leader that there has been a notable increase in the challenges of ego that people are facing. This makes perfect sense. Our group consciousness has come together on a universal level to rise up and explore the issues of ego (raising hell, you might say).

The individual illusion that we are separate from God takes form in the ego. As stated before, the ego is a necessary part of our journey and has been our protector in a world of survival, keeping us alive as a human race, to reach this point where we are now free to explore ourselves as a spiritual race. As we look at the universal consciousness, we take this ego to another level. I have seen it as the addiction entity (others call it the devil, Satan . . . you know the names). It is a massive tumor-like energy that begins to vibrate out of sync with the Creator God's energy of love. It is an insatiable desire of all things primitive. I have seen it and faced it many times, and other seers I know have described it in the same way (as have many artists throughout time). A large, black, scaly creature with red eyes, it comes in from behind and crawls its way into the mind. It feeds off of fear, pain, greed, guilt, and anger, but it is never satisfied, and so it is always hungry, coaxing those energies from whoever is open to its call. Its true craving, however, is for love and joy, which is why it is never satisfied by these lower vibrating energies, leaving it constantly preying (praying) for more.

With masses of people exploring their own egos at the same time, the group ego consciousness is flaring up all around in a desperate ploy for survival. It is taking many forms, and light workers across the world have been challenged by its call. It is our job to remember that *everything is of God* and that this separateness is just an illusion. We must not fight the ego on an individual or group level but rather stand still in the Heart Center and welcome it to us with love. We must remember that, while ego (both individual and universal) feeds off of these lower moving vibrations, its true desire is its reunion with the energy of God's love. That is what we must offer this red-eyed monster when it shows itself to us.

In a previous chapter, I told the story of the Iroquois Peacemaker. This story is a beautiful illustration of the role of the ego. I tell it again here in that context. The story speaks of Hiawatha (the emotional self), a violent warrior who accepted the message of peace from the Peacemaker, a messenger of the Creator (the I Am presence, God Self, or Higher Power). Having received the truth of the Creator's love, Hiawatha went forward to spread the news to others, only to be faced with the "evil sorcerer," the Tadadaho (ego). The Tadadaho ruled the people with fear. He was said to have seven crooks in his back (seven closed chakras) and snakes in his hair. The Tadadaho, seeing Hiawatha's message of peace as a threat to his power, killed all of Hiawatha's children. Hiawatha, of course, was devastated and wandered away from the Peacemaker in his grief. Eventually, the Peacemaker came to him and offered him a grieving ceremony in which he cleansed the tears from his eyes so he could see truth again, his ears so he could hear truth again, and his throat so he could once again speak words of love. The Peacemaker (higher self) then instructed Hiawatha (emotional self) to approach the Tadadaho (ego self) with a song of love. As the Peacemaker and Hiawatha sang a song of love to the Tadadaho, they combed the snakes from his hair and straightened the crooks in his back (healing the body to receive the flow of the Creator's energy). After the Tadadaho (ego self) was healed with love, he was instructed that he would be the one to lead the people as long as he was aligned with the love of the Creator. Even today, the Tadadaho remains in the position of Chief of the Iroquois Nations.

This union of the ego, the emotional self, and the spiritual self into one complete consciousness is the journey that we as a world are walking today. Many individuals have stepped up to embrace this remembrance within their own personal journey. Many others who have already awakened and aligned to this truth have been called to face the ego and to hold it with love in service to others. I give great honor to all those who are standing in the center of this illusion of the "battle between the ego and the spirit." Whether on an individual or a universal level, our quest to see beyond the illusion and to love beyond understanding is the gift we give to the world. It is what will bring peace to our planet, and it is the end of the illusion of addiction and suffering and the beginning of a new vibrant Earth.

≈ 5 ≈

Partnership

*In the embrace of Enchanted One, I open my heart com-
pletely and without limit. I move forward with the flow of
divine love in all of my relationships and embrace the joy
of passion on Earth.*

≈

In order to love others we must first love ourselves. We
must find our connection to our divine source of love
and center ourselves in that peaceful wisdom. This takes
a deep and passionate exploration of ourselves. It often
means looking at the past, releasing our emotions, and
exploring our belief systems. Someone once told me she
was "dating herself." I thought that was beautiful. To
engage in a love affair with oneself, to explore who one
is, and to take time to nurture and romance oneself is a
wonderful concept. I think we all need to find time to do
this in our lives.

The journey of love is *always* a journey between
our self and our divine source. This, however, does not
mean that it should be done in the absence of the people

around us. I often tell people that to truly embrace love as humans, we must come down from the mountain and enjoy the campfire.

At some point in our lifetimes, most of us have tasted enlightenment—in a church, perhaps, or an ashram, or up on a mountaintop secluded from society. Most of us, in a single moment during meditation, prayer, yoga, or worship, have had a moment of blissful grace in which we have felt completely centered and connected to All That Is. This is often experienced in solitude, but as humans we are social beings. The goal is to achieve this place of grace and unconditional love with each other. And, as we now know, that begins with ourselves. The irony and the beauty in this paradox is that it is through our relationships with others that we are given endless opportunities to experience a deeper love for ourselves.

When Magdalene and Isis were explaining it, the phrase very specifically came not as "and," and not as "in," but as "n" . . . "peace 'n passion in partnership"— not only peace and passion but also peace *in* passion. The concept that they are referring to is the learning that happens when we have passion about ourselves, passion about our work, passion about our relationships, passion about our children, passion about our spiritual journey. Passion is the place from which we are driven. From a place of passion comes the whole spectrum of emotions, including anger, fear, compassion, love, and joy. It is the idea of being open to the emotions.

People are seeking peace. When we go on a solitary journey to find peace, peace comes from our union with the Creator. Peace doesn't mean necessarily that we sit on the top of a mountain and say "ohm," with an inner tranquility that is not affected by the outside because we are able to meditate for large amounts of time. Yes, that is a journey, and we probably all took it in one of our lifetimes, when we were a monk or a nun or a priest or someone who could remove themselves from the world and just work on their individual relationship with the Creator. But we are also on this journey to seal our connections with the Creator within us, even—and especially—in our relationships, in the workforce, and in the context of our daily lives. There is an internal journey to peace, an internal journey to passion on our spiritual path, but there is also an *external* journey, which is why we come to Earth. This journey is why we want to experience partnerships, the whole essence of being here on Earth, because we can touch, we can feel emotions, we can see, we can breathe, we can smell, and we can hear.

These interrelationships with the physical world are why we come to Earth, so that we can have those five senses and experience them. And a lot of times, we get frustrated with our own journey. We're seeking our connection back to remembering our Oneness with the Creator, and we get angry with the Earth experience because it is interfering with that. But when we seal that union, and we remember that union, then we also remember why we are here.

We're here to touch, to smell, to hear, to breathe, to feel, to taste all of those things that are related, interrelationships, soul relationships, connected in a physical way, in an emotional way that we can't have on the other side. If you think about losing someone you love, even if you have the gift of knowing your spiritual connection with them, of talking to them, of sensing them, you still grieve them. Why? What are you grieving? You're grieving the ability to touch, to laugh, to see their face, to hear their laughter, to hear their song, to hear their voice, to just be present in that partnership on a physical level. You're grieving the ability to experience them on the level of your senses.

"Divine partnerships" is a term that Magdalene offered me years ago to describe the journey of soulmates on Earth. In her wonderful way of dissecting words, she expressed this as divine partner-Ships, giving me an image of two ships on an ocean blue. She showed these ships traveling to the same destination. They were on the same blue water, heading in the same direction, and they had decided together the final destination (the God Center). Two ships traveling in the same direction will not always take the exact same course. As the winds shift and cast upon the sails of each ship, there will be times when they travel very closely together and times when they will appear to be heading in opposite directions.

Trusting in the journey and not needing to tether to each other in the moment is what allows both ships to journey together to their destination. If the ships focus their attention on staying together rather than trusting in the fullness of the journey, they will hold each other back and will not reach their destination. In fact, if they completely tether to each other, they will come to a standstill and the same winds that once carried them will push them to beat against each other in the current, destroying both vessels with time. But when the ships are left to their own journey, they will have moments of incredible closeness where they can enjoy the details of each other's presence, and they will have times of distance where they can take in the full beauty of the other vessel, the journey, the water, the sky, and the destination's approach. In truth, we should strive to transform all of our relationships into divine partnerships. No matter what form a partnership takes, living in divine partnership is an act of unconditional love. Striving to love unconditionally in all of our relationships is our goal.

It is so important that we're working on the physical level. Romance is only one form of intimate soul connection, only one piece of it. Any type of friendship, any co-working together, any passion about a certain career service that you could be a part of—all of these things create those energies, and they in turn give space to emotion. When you become passionate about something, you open yourself up to all of the emotions: to joy, to jealousy, to love, to compassion, to fear, to anger. It's not "controlled" like when you stay within yourself, sealed in solitude. Sometimes people who don't want the spiritual journey don't want that peace because they think it is too quiet. But when you *truly* take the spiritual journey, which includes passion, you will experience the full spectrum of emotions and at the same time keep an inner core of peace. Even as you are experiencing all of the passion of anger, and love, and joy, even as the outer world seems to move at a rapid emotional tempo, your inner core will know peace.

You can have peaceful moments, quiet moments in relationships where you can learn just as much as the more loud, "passionate" people, so that you have both the peace *and* the passion. Even when you're deeply angry or deeply grieving, or even deeply joyful, you can also have this center core of peace, of knowing that this is something you're experiencing at the moment, seeing the bigger picture and knowing everything is divine. You can then *use* that emotion, use its positive aspects to impact the movement of your life. So anger can become, "I'm so angry that I'm going to *do* something about this," or "I'm so angry that I'm going to speak my voice and say what I need to say to claim my truth": Sometimes the emotions you are feeling are serving as springboards to the passion that will allow you to create your life, to manifest the life that you want.

∾

Isis Speaks on Peace 'n Passion

My beloved children of peace and joy, of passion and life, of touch and laughter: Look into yourselves. You are beautiful. You are the perfect expression of the Creator. Do you forget this? Do you forget the honor of your journey? Do you forget that only the most beautiful souls journey to the depth of this emotion? Remember now, my children, for you have journeyed long. You have journeyed among the villages for so long you have forgotten where you came from. Remember now.

Remember that you have within you, that you have brought with you everything that you need for this journey. Remember that you came down from the mountain to experience the passions of life. It was your heart that called you here; follow your heart. Your heart will lead you back up the mountain, but not until you have mastered what it came to learn, so open to that. When you got down to the bottom of the mountain, did you not fear? Did that fear not scare you? Did you not feel anger, and did that not scare you? Did you not shut the crevices of your heart that led you here? You shut the roadmap back; do you see that? In your desire to control these emotions, you shut the very place in you that remembered, that led you, that leads you to the expanded understanding on top of the mountain. Open those crevices now, and allow them to come in.

This can be experienced on your own, yes, but it is in partnership that you have mirrors. We do not speak only of that which you would call romantic partnership. Yes, that is a beautiful vibration, it is a vibration that expands you to the deepest parts of your essence; this is true. But it is only one fragment, and when you put all your attention on that you miss so much of the lesson.

Love of self is one thing, but to look into the vibration of another as a reflection expands that love. That is our origin, and from that many of you understand that we moved more and more in that expansion-ness so that we could understand more and more of this journey. Just as you took this journey down from the mountain this time, you have done so many times. You have done it many times, and have redone it, and you were us. We are all One.

Trust in your journey; trust in these gifts of emotion. Follow them through, and we tell you that you will follow them through to love, for that is all there is. Each one of these emotions, whether you seek it or run from it, each is an expression of love in divine form, of compassion. That is what is underneath each of them. Open to them in relationship, in partnership. Each relationship, each person that you relate to, is an opportunity for you to journey into the deepest part of your soul, for you to open the gateways of joy, of love, all of the gateways, no matter what emotion that gate is being held by. Allow it now, trusting in the divine love, trusting in your acceptance of peace to remain in that spot, trusting that you are on the mountain, that you are a piece of God, that you *are* God, and that you are merely taking this journey to learn, to grow, to expand in your love.

And when you come across a soul that reflects emotions, sometimes that feels out of control. They are so passionate, in one form or another. Do not run from these emotions; open your heart to them until you find harmony in them, for there is no greater purpose on Earth than to open to the touch, to the feel of the emotional plane. That is your bridge between the physical and the spiritual. That is where peace is found. But peace is not the numbness that so many speak of. Peace is not excluding yourself from the journey. Peace is not delay. Peace is embracing the journey to the end and knowing that even as you embrace this journey you already have the peace and divine love inside of you—you merely choose to understand it in this deeper form.

—*Isis, as channeled through Sheila*

⁓ 6 ⁓

Male/Female: Releasing the Illusion

Enchanted One ~ Alpha and Omega within me, I embrace now the fullness of all that I am. Remembering the God and the Goddess within me, I release now all illusion of separateness that keeps me from loving passionately on Earth.

⁓

Wake Up, Sleeping Beauty

Sleeping Beauty, Snow White, and Cinderella have all been asleep and suppressed for too long. The feminine aspect of the Creator within us has been lost to the overpowering male vibration. This is not a feminist statement. It has nothing to do with the male or female form of the body. Everyone has within them the Alpha and the Omega. The Alpha, which is also known as the male vibration, is the more logical, assertive, and linear energy, the thought. The Omega is known as the female vibration, and this holds the emotional, gentle, and circular energy, the receptor. The harmonic union of the mind and the emotion is creation, thought made manifest.

Not only have females been removed from the power of religions and governments, but the value of the female energy of creation has been suppressed within each of us. It is time for the princess in all of us to wake up. The celebration of the Goddess energy within our Creator and each of us as individuals is a necessary component of creating the fully abundant, joyful, and loving life we desire. The harmonic union of the feminine and masculine aspects of Life is at the core of every spiritual journey. However, historically, the feminine aspects of our Creator and ourselves have been suppressed. It is the fear of the incredible power of this harmonic union of the God/Goddess that has led to its suppression.

One of the first steps in realigning the Alpha and Omega energies is to celebrate the Goddess energy within all of us. This Goddess energy has been suppressed for so long that it must be celebrated and understood in order for it to return to a harmonic state with the male aspect of Creation. Regardless of one's physical composition as male or female in any particular lifetime, when one fully aligns with the harmonic union of the God/Goddess energy within the soul, he or she will have aligned with the Creation energy. From this space, one can create a completely abundant life of love and joy. Each individual who moves into this harmonic balance of Creation assists in his or her own personal journey. The alignment of these two forces within the individual adds new perception to the Universal Mind, leading to the harmonic union of the God/Goddess energy within all of Mother Earth.

The journey to your awakening is both within and without. You are both the prince and the princess. To honor the princess in you, you must go deep within.

Learn who you are through meditation, dreams, and the help of spirit guides. Remain determined to love and to hold onto what you know to be true, regardless of what the world is telling you. Seek the place deep in your heart where you are connected to love and truth. When the miracles come, take a risk. To love and be loved must become your greatest dream, to see beauty in all people and to remain pure even when others treat you in unjust and unloving ways. Your Goddess self has been asleep, untainted by the harshness of the elements. Wake her up. Choose to love and to be the expression of love. This is a choice, and when you choose, the spiritual world, nature, animals, and spirit guides come to give you all that you need. Make your commitment to opening your eyes and trusting All That Is. Celebrate and embrace these aspects. Kiss the princess in you, and let her dance.

To honor the prince within you, who is fearlessly and relentlessly seeking the purity, the princess, in every situation, you make your quest to live the expression of unconditional love. You will encounter many obstacles and barriers. Remember, our society has spent a terrific amount of time suppressing the feelings of vulnerability that unconditional love evokes in us. Just by living on Earth, you have been subject to the conditioning that love is about meeting the needs of survival. On your journey to true unconditional love, you will be faced not only with society's barriers but also your own. You will believe the illusions of walls. You will be conditioned to see thorns rather than roses, and you will face many challenges on your own journey as prince to awaken the princess inside of you. You must be diligent to see each situation from a new perspective, to call on your spirit guides to help you. Your quest to awaken the Goddess

Within must summon the source of strength to overcome all obstacles.

All of the personal work that we do to heal ourselves and find our center is in essence simply about waking up, releasing the illusion, and remembering that we are already whole and perfect reflections of God's love on Earth. Once we begin to remember, we can step out of the illusion of the karmic cycle and embrace the journey of Oneness in ourselves and in all our relations.

Part II

Embracing Emotions

≈ 7 ≈

The Gifts

I rest into the Heart Center, flooding myself with the vibration of divine love that we are. In this space I embrace the full spectrum of emotions as a gift on my journey to remembering Enchanted One.

≈

A wakening to the understanding that we are part of this great Oneness that is All That Is, and at the same time that we are on Earth to experience the illusion of separateness to explore emotions, is a paradox. How do we embrace Oneness and the illusion at the same time? The answer lies in our learning to be both the observer and the participant in each moment. From this place of full knowing, we can choose to place our attention either on the experience of the individual "cell" that is our current form and circumstance, or to put our attention on the whole Being that is our Oneness with God.

The other day, a very grounded friend who is a self-proclaimed skeptic reported to me that he had had a "strange day." The entire day had felt like a dream, and even during a conversation with a friend he had had to "remind [himself] that [he] was not in a dream." What he was experiencing was an awakening to the illusion. In those moments, he had been both the observer and the participant in his life. I laughed and said, "Welcome to my world! I think you will like it here!" He replied, "The jury is still out on that; it was a bit unnerving." Interesting choice of words: "Unnerving" is exactly what it was; in those moments, he had released his grip on being attached to the illusion of the physical experience and was beginning to expand himself to the wholeness of All That Is. He was moving his awareness from the single focus of the central nervous system that makes up his physical experience and expanding that awareness to the central God Center that makes up the universe. This is our goal: To become both the wholeness of God and the singleness of human in the same moment.

I live in an 1830s farmhouse. The basement of this house is built of dirt, stone, and trees. As a result, it is damp, dirty, and filled with cobwebs and who knows what else, and so, for the most part, I avoid it at all costs. In fact, I usually only go down there when I have blown a fuse, which happens when I have been attempting to do too many things at once without paying attention to the connectedness of it all. However, when my children were little, they used to put on their wellie boots, grab a flashlight, and go on great adventures down there. They called it treasure hunting. Exploring the unknown is fun when we are children. In reality, this basement of ours, once you look past its dark dankness, is a wonderful place. You can actually see the axe marks from where the beams were chopped and the stones that were carried and stacked by hand to create a family homestead. It is a wonderful expression of history.

Throughout time, people have used the basement as a metaphor for our unconscious, our unexplored psyche, and our base chakra. This is the place within us where we dump our unfelt emotions, hiding in the dark crevices the parts of us that we do not want to look at. We work to avoid this space, and we attempt to keep the light out. Exploring emotions allows us to bring light to these dark spaces of our psyche and restore beauty to our life. Once we learn to navigate this space, we become joyful explorers on this journey of humanness. Once we understand what our core fear is, we can begin to explore the spectrum of emotions we have been so afraid to address.

Our core fear is not of the emotions themselves; rather, it is of the power within us to affect the universe, and so we transfer that fear instead to our emotions and become prisoners in our own bodies. It is only after truly understanding and being willing to release this core fear that we can finally get down to the business of exploring the world of emotions we are here to master. Let us begin this journey together now.

~

A Message from Isis

When this journey began, it was with the pull of the heart . . . not the illusion of separation, but the pull of the heart to expand our understanding. And we say to you, when we were in such power and we expanded to experience emotions of greed and fear, jealousy and anger, love and attraction, a passionate deep romance, deep unconditional love, we too did not understand how to work with all of this expansion-ness. We were the ones that initiated the closing down, for in our power of understanding, our lack of understanding, it was huge. And as you are each cells of us, as you are each part of the whole, these fears do not come from you, they come from evolution.

This fear of emotion, this fear of living passionately, comes from the original point where it felt out of control. The human race has tried to control and to control and to control for so many generations, and the Earth has experienced this vibration. And now the Earth is in a part of evolution that is all it knows, and that is all it remembers . . . for this brief moment, that is the vibration of Earth. But we say to you, cycle back, do not be afraid of emotions, for it is the emotions that have brought you here. Do not be afraid to experience them, for you have brought yourselves to a point where it is safe. This is why we have reduced ourselves to such tiny specks in our understanding of this expansion, so that we can build back up.

Each time you experience an emotion, you help to rebuild our existence. Each time you look into another soul and feel love, feel anger, feel joy, feel fear, *allow* yourself to feel it, because we say to you that if you do, you allow yourself to take that journey in peace and understanding that you are all okay, you are encircled by God. You cannot hurt, you cannot destroy that which is God . . . there is nothing that you can destroy.

There is deepness in having compassion for the stranger on the street, for having compassion for the one that hurt you the most, the one that seems so strong that it overbears you. Passion . . . love . . . first, you must experience those emotions that you avoid, for if you have anger at one who dominates you, or fear at one who triggers you, and you choose not to experience this, you are not finding peace, you are finding numbness . . . you are shutting yourself down, not opening yourself up. The enlightened one is one that experiences all emotions and takes joy in the experience of them. Even in the deepest grief, there is joy in knowing that the soul is expanding in its understanding, in its vastness. There is joy and love in the anger, in knowing that the body has experienced something as a trigger of passion, something that fell out of vibration so that the soul can bring it into vibration, in line with the passion, the desire of manifestation.

Why do you get angry? You get angry because something doesn't feel aligned with your truth. Do not sit in it, but do not suppress it. Be aware of it so that you can use it to understand your truth. It is merely a tool . . . all of these emotions are tools; they're gifts. They are gifts. They are gifts.

I speak to you of this from great experience. I speak to you of this because I have journeyed hard to understand this myself, being one of the souls that has expanded from God, being one of the vibration. There are so many stories to explain this evolution—it doesn't matter what the name—but the truth, the truth in remembering the initial expansion—not separation but expansion—of the God Center, expansion of All That Is into the God and Goddess vibration, the Alpha and Omega that was there to experience love, the truth is what matters.

—Isis, *as channeled through Sheila*

Fear

*Enchanted One ~ Wrap me with the power of divine love
as I sit in the fire of fear. Open my heart to receive the gifts
of transformation that await me beyond my illusions.*

≈

Whether we look at the universe, apart from human
beings, all of nature, for the most part, lives in
the trust that the universe will provide for it; it simply
serves the purpose that it is here for. A deer is a deer;
a dog, a dog. They are not trying to be something else;
they are simply being what they are. And on some level,
as humans, that is what we are trying to return to. Survival is a part of our nature: We want to live comfortably
on Earth, provide for our family, and protect the lives of
the ones we care for. And sometimes we fear not having those needs met. When we fear this, we are truly in
the illusion of the separation because in that moment we
believe we are not fully cared for.

We humans have explored our "reality" to a level
that now allows us to have free thought and to make vast

decisions, and we really have learned to control our environment in ways that other species have not. We have the ability to think in abstract ways, to communicate with each other, to travel around the world. We have evolved to a space where we can experience many wonderful things. And yet, with this evolution has come an innate fear that we are not okay, that we are not enough. We are as afraid of the idea of not being taken care of as we are of the idea that we have the ability to have everything, that maybe we truly are powerful.

While we look at these fears of powerlessness and powerfulness, it seems that they are on opposite sides of the spectrum. But we can think instead of a ring of fire around us, a ring that is both fear *and* passion, realizing they are the same biological expression. There is one continuous fear in us that we are separate from God, from All That Is, from the Creator, and at the same time a fear that we are God and therefore extremely powerful, with all the responsibility that implies. If we are separate, then we may not be taken care of and we may not have the ability to do what we need to do for ourselves, our family, or the world. In waking up from that fear, our fear now becomes the other extreme: Maybe we *are* powerful, maybe we have within our hands the ability to create the life we desire, maybe happiness *is* reachable on Earth and not just after death.

Over the centuries, people have separated God from humanness. This occurred when we created the concept of heaven above and Earth below. This separation creates an innate conflict within us: We are seeking a God and a life in heaven, where everything will be provided for, a peace that will come to us after death. And at the exact same time we are living on Earth, implanted with this ego, this innate primitive survival instinct. Our human nature tells us to survive as humans, which means to resist that "tunnel of light" that comes when we die, while at the same time we teach that true happiness only comes with death. And so it is, that the one thing that we are afraid of is the very thing that we are reaching for.

This convoluted cycle creates a ring of fear around us from which there is no way out. Either we are weak and that is scary or we are powerful and that is scary. We start moving toward one end of the fire, feel the burning, and then move to the center. Then we go toward the other side, feel the burning, and move to the center. We are stuck in this ring of fear until we realize that the ring is exactly what saves us: The ability to move through it is the very ability that allows us to be okay in every single situation. When we face our fears, when we align with our higher self, moving towards that fear and allowing ourselves to experience fear without resistance, we come to realize that this emotion does not have any more power than any other energy that is around us. We learn that we can simply be in the emotion of fear and allow it to move over us so that we can continue on our journey. In this sense, the ring of fear simply ceases to exist after we have allowed it to serve its purpose of burning away the conflict of remembering our Oneness and the fear of being separate.

There is nothing separate from God, and therefore our fears cannot be separate from God. To resist our fears is to resist God. When we move to expand ourselves, in some way we are moving toward the light and the primitive instinct inside of us comes up to protect us. If we don't listen to it, it is going to get louder and will play itself out in our mind and in our body until we do. Simply stop in that moment of fear, and listen. Listen to that part of yourself that is saying, "Don't go into the light." Hear it, validate it, discover the truth in its message, and then explain it the new way. You will continue to feel this conflict until you embrace that part of yourself that you have been resisting, acknowledge it, listen to it, and bring it into alignment with your higher consciousness. This is what is meant by bringing the head and the heart into alignment. Your fears are a gift, and you want to pay attention and then evaluate the new circumstance.

The new circumstance is that heaven is coming down to Earth. It is safe to lose yourself, to expand into something more. The old patterns have brought us so far. Those beliefs have kept us alive as a human race, but they are not going to take us to the next phase, which is to bring that light and remember that light here on Earth. In this space, we are living in our full expansive self. Fear is a part of us because we are all One, so if we do not acknowledge this part of us, if we do not allow ourselves to listen to it and feel it without attaching to it, it stays with us. We want instead to convert it into the fire of passion, and the way we convert it is by taking the power out of the fear, allowing ourselves to experience it, feel it, understand it, and then simply move on.

≈ 9 ≈

Grief

In the aching of my heart I find the throbbing pulse of the divine. For in the depth of my grief is the remembrance of my union . . . the knowing that love never ends. Enchanted One, hold me as I journey into the depth of my grief to discover that love has never left me.

~

Fear and avoidance of grief rules our relationships. We guard ourselves against love, for fear of losing love. But, in fact, love never ends. We can never lose love, not through distance, not through divorce, not even through death. Love never ends. When we remember this, we are free to allow love into our lives in each moment.

What is it we are grieving when we perceive the loss of someone we love? We are grieving the touch, the feeling, the moments, the memories, the hopes, the perceptions, and even the projections. When we stay in each moment, we cannot feel grief because we know that we are whole and that love never leaves; it may change forms, but it never leaves. The problem is that we are human, and so staying in the moment is a very difficult task. We are constantly exploring the timeline, projecting our thoughts into the future and lingering in memories of the past. But it is in this space of "holding on" to a form or a moment or an ideal that we encounter grief, because love is ever moving and cannot be held to any single moment. It is important to know this, and yet it is also important to allow ourselves the luxury of that grief. We are human. We came here to explore emotion, and so explore we must.

I remember coming to the realization that my marriage was changing forms. I tried so hard to cling to what we had had: I cried at each holiday, thinking it would be the last one we would spend together; I thought of the joy we had had in the past, and I cried; I thought of all the times I would not have my husband by my side, and I cried. What I was really grieving was the form of our relationship. I was letting go of who we had been in the past; I was releasing all the ideals I had gathered regarding what marriage should look like. In truth, however, I lost neither my friend nor my memories of the past. We still go hiking, we still travel together, we still raise our children in partnership together. He is still there when I need a shoulder to cry on, and six years later we still spend at least part of most holidays together. So what was I grieving? The illusion. But it was important to grieve that because, in doing so, I opened the space for the love in the relationship to continue to flow its natural course. Had I not taken the time to feel that loss, the emotions would have come out in other ways, creating a barrier between us. Had we clung to the ideal of how we thought our relationship was meant to go, we would have inadvertently suppressed each other's truth and in time we would have resented each other.

Traditionally, society has not supported the ever-changing flow of unconditional love in partnership. We enter partnerships, especially marriages, with expectations of the form those relationships will take over time. If we do not allow the adjustment of form with the ever-transforming flow of unconditional love, it is easy to feel like a victim when our relationship changes in ways we do not expect. When our relationships change form unexpectedly, grieving the form we expected our relationship to take is still essential. There are five stages of grief, and it is important for us to honor ourselves as we move through each of those phases: denial, bargaining, anger, sadness, and acceptance. Acknowledging our process in each stage allows us to move forward in divine love.

Grieving the form of the relationship I had had with my husand was important and allowed us both to embrace the changing form of our love. The same thing happens when a loved one dies: we grieve that life; we grieve the touch, the laughter, the physical form of the relationship; we long for the past; and we grieve dreams that will never come to form. But if we allow ourselves the purging of those feelings, they will begin to lift, and love itself will fill the space that is left.

Deep grief is not unfamiliar to me. Previously, I mentioned my beloved's crossing over to the spirit world after being hit by a drunk driver. His passage was easy and unlike any I had experienced before: He stepped between the realms with simplicity and grace. When I expressed concern to my daughter that she was not showing her grief, she said to me, "Tom never left me—doesn't anyone get that?" She was right. He has continued to journey with us as he always had. He is a part of our daily life, and we all see, hear, and feel his support. He also continues to work with me as I teach the world about love. Our dedication, our spiritual union, the time that we spent uniting on the spiritual level—even when he was here on Earth in body—were key to our ability to love beyond this life. But this did not stop the emotions of grief. They were intense, and when I was feeling them sometimes I could not feel him. Why? Because I was living in the past, trying to cling to the memories of how things had been.

The thing with grief is that, like every emotion, when we suppress the feeling it does not go, but lingers. When we first open our hearts to such a depth of pain, it can feel overwhelming: We are feeling all the unfelt grief and pain that our soul has experienced from the beginning of time, and while we are stuck in the illusion of separateness, that pain can feel insurmountable. However, as we awaken to the remembrance of our Oneness with All That Is, we begin to realize that even pain is an illusion. In this space, we allow ourselves the experience of the emotion at the same time that we continue to be embraced by love. There is no doubt in my mind or heart that my beloved twin flame is still with me: He is me; we are one. I know this in every fiber of my being. Most days, I feel whole and complete in our Oneness, and then there are days when, for whatever reason, I choose to experience the illusion of separateness, and grief pours from me. But as it leaves, love spills into the emptiness and my wholeness deepens. Love never ends, not even in death, because love is all there is. If we allow ourselves this understanding, we will have the faith to open our hearts to love in every form.

⇒ 10 ⇐

Anger

I greet my anger with love . . . listening with an open heart as my anger rises from the depths of my emotions and transforms to passion. I am awakening. I pour gratitude into my anger for the piercing remembrance of Enchanted One's passionate embrace.

Fierce love transforms all of me to All That Is.

~

For many of us, anger is the most frightening emotion of all. When we anger, we are in passion. If we did not care about the person or situation that evoked our anger, we would not have been triggered; therefore, like every emotion, anger is an expression of love. It may not necessarily be the expression we want to live in often, but it is an expression of love nonetheless.

I once had a friend who shut me out of his life for three years. During those years, he convinced himself that he hated me. When he finally reconnected with me, my response to him was, "I take it as a compliment that you had to feel such anger in order to stay away from me;

if you didn't love me so much, you wouldn't have had to believe you hated me." He agreed, and we continued the friendship on a new level.

Anger is love in fear. All emotions come down to either love or fear. When we are centered in Oneness, we feel passionate love; when we are in the illusion of separateness and feel passion, it is anger. This is very important to understand, because anger is one of the core emotions that we struggle with. When we do not acknowledge anger, when we do not learn how to express it in a healthy way, we turn it inward and it becomes cancer. Yes, I did just say that. Cancer is anger turned inward. If we learn to embrace anger, centering in the Oneness of divine love and letting that love align every cell of our body, cancer will no longer exist. There is no need for it to exist in the Oneness. Cancer is simply cells vibrating out of alignment with the body. We are cells of God, and when we are in the illusion of separateness, embracing love as fear and anger, we are vibrating out of alignment with the Oneness of God's vessel. At the core, our anger is our anger at God, or, more specifically, at the illusion of separateness. Anger is love in fear.

There is one primary reason we are afraid of our anger: we are afraid God has abandoned us. We are afraid we are being punished in this illusion of time and space because of what we have created in anger. At the same time, we are afraid that we are not abandoned, that we are part of the wholeness of God and are capable of and meant to create with our emotions. And then we are afraid again: If we create in anger, we will destroy the things we love. But love never ends! Everything is God. Nothing can be created or destroyed. All That Is is love. We have to align with the memory of this truth in order to allow ourselves the experience of anger on Earth. When we get to the core, when we realize that what we are really angry at is the God we perceive abandoned us and the part of us that believes this illusion, then we release our true anger and the soul that we are begins to vibrate once again in alignment with All That Is. In this space, we are free to experience anger in its various forms, to allow it into us and watch it transform into passionate love.

Once again, anger is an emotion that most of us have suppressed for a long time, and so when we first start opening to this emotion we may feel a bit overwhelmed by the experience. Remembering to use spiritual techniques like meditation, prayer, and dreamwork helps. It is also helpful to use the body via exercise. Anger is one of our most primitive ego-based emotions; it was intended to help us survive when our life was being threatened. When my twin flame was alive on Earth, as wonderful as he was with my children, there were times when he would provoke them, which would trigger me. I used to say to him, "Mama bear is coming out," which meant, "Watch out because my instinct is to protect my children." Even though I knew they were not in danger, the notion that they were being threatened in some way made me fierce. This is the ego again, the primitive part of ourselves that is programmed to keep our species alive on Earth.

The passion that comes from deep, unconditional love (as in a mama's love for her children), which is God's light on Earth, triggers our instinctual primitive emotions of anger (the "mama bear" response). And so, by embracing anger and acknowledging it, we create a space to transform it once again into the passionate love that will allow us to move forward into our Oneness.

∽ 11 ∾

Jealousy

*I open my heart to Enchanted One, remembering that all
is divine. Love never ends. There is an endless flow of love
always. When jealousy rises within me I remind my ego
that we are one.*

∿

L ike anger, jealousy is an expression of love that is
based in fear and lack. Again, love never ends. Love
is All That Is, and therefore there is an infinite flow of
love available to us. God has not abandoned us. When
we are in the flow of that, knowing that *all* of our needs
will be met—that what one person has we all have, since
we are one—then the more abundance, love, and joy on
Earth there is available for us to tap into.

When we are jealous of the things people have or
the lives they seem to be living, we are seeing only the
shell; we are assuming that somehow the universe has
blessed them in a way in which we ourselves have not
been blessed. But in truth, we are responsible for the life
we have. In every situation, we can choose either love or

fear; we can choose to align with the flow of Creation or to align with the illusion of separation. This is what creates our reality. When we are jealous, we are aligned with separation. In that space, we believe in a limited supply of love and abundance, and we feel threatened that someone is taking our share. And yet what we truly seek is that union with God where we feel whole and supported by the flow of love in every moment.

Jealousy is perhaps most ramped up in our "romantic relationships." This is because it is in this space that we are truly dancing with the idea of Oneness with God. When we surrender to someone in sacred sexual love, we come close to tasting the feeling of expansion that comes with remembering our union with the universal flow of divine love. We want this experience so badly that we do everything we can to hold onto it. This is why we have put so many rules around the form of romantic/sexual love.

Most people spend the majority of their lives seeking this union, reading about it, watching movies about it, and attempting to live in it. And yet at the same time, we put just as much effort into confining it. We create rules to give us the illusion it will be safe. But while these rules create the illusion of safety, they also reduce the possibility of love. Women are jealous of women, men of men, single people of married people, and married people of single people because everyone is focusing on the form of the love rather than the love itself. They feel the limits of the form they have created and believe that another form will work better, or they are so attached to the form they are in that they no longer feel the flow of love in the moment.

Some people are so frightened that the form of their relationship will change that they live in fear rather than love. They cannot actually embrace the love they have in their relationship because they are clinging so tightly to the past, to that initial feeling of love they felt when they first came together, or they are clinging to the idea of what love will feel like in the future when all their earthly needs are met. But love is in the moment. It is not in the past or the future—it is in the present.

To feel jealousy is an indication to us that we are living in the illusion of separateness. We are believing in that moment that we must cling to our love; we are believing in the lie that we can lose love. When we are aligned with the flow of love, we are embracing the knowledge that in that moment no one can take that away from us. When we allow the love in our relationships to flow, it creates in each moment the perfect form of that love, and that endless flow of love's embrace will be perfect not only for us but for everyone around us.

Love begets love. When we allow love to flow in our lives, we are never at risk of losing anyone. We honor the perfect reflection of our love in every moment and allow others the freedom to do the same. The presence of jealousy serves as an opportunity to remind us to ungrip our clenched fist and allow love to flow once again in its beautiful perfection.

☞ 12 ☜

Lust

Enchanted One ~ In the embrace of divine love I accept all of me. Every human feeling is an expression of All That Is. Pouring divine love into my physical desires, I embrace the power of sacred creation energy. In this space, I am free to co-create now all of my desires with love.

∼

In the most primitive sense, creation energy is an insatiable desire for all things tactile, and lust for all things physical is the instinctual desire to keep the human race alive. We crave food, drink, adventure, and sex. These are the human survival instincts.

Fortunately, as a species, we have moved beyond just the survival mode. However, we must remember that our physiological makeup is still programmed to survive and procreate. When we acknowledge this reality and then align with the expanded understanding that we are more than just our physical beings, we can embrace the human experience while transforming our primitive desires to include our sacred desires as well.

Our basic need to survive makes us crave food, drink, sex, and exercise. Once we meet those needs, we can allow love to flow into that space. We can engage in social activities while meeting those needs, and we can embrace more than just our primitive needs in every given moment. Beyond the body, we are sustained by love itself. In truth, there is no need to eat or drink or breathe, for that matter. However, we are choosing to stay in the illusion of Earth life and physical form even after we awaken to the knowing of Oneness. And as long as we put our consciousness on our physical life, we can strive to expand beyond our primitive physical needs and transform even the most basic instinctual survival behaviors into expressions of love.

Why are we so afraid of our primitive instincts for sex? Because on some level we understand that within this primitive desire to procreate is Creation itself. When we align with the Creator and allow the full expression of the endless flow of love into our sexual lives, when love and lust meet and the sacredness of the soul dances in union with the physical, we ourselves become Creators! And in this space, we have the power to create all our desires.

We have created many rules around our feelings of lust because we are so frightened of the power that lies within that Creation energy. It is time for us as a human race to move beyond our fears, to embrace our sexual nature and to infuse it with the love of Creation in order to regain the sacred power that is inherent in the core of the sacred union of man and God.

⇜ 13 ⇝

Joy

Pink bubbling joy rising from the depth of my heart and pouring into the world around me is the greatest gift I can give humanity. Divine love, fill me on my journey that I may choose joy as my service to our world.

∽

Joy is an interesting emotion. Most people probably think they are searching for joy, and most people would probably deny that they are afraid of joy. But think about it. How many times have you heard the words, "too good to be true," or "waiting for the other shoe to drop?" We may be seeking joy, but most people don't actually trust it.

Most people are afraid to surrender into the joy in front of them. We are, once again, so afraid to let go into the flow of love, so afraid that we are being punished and that God has abandoned us, that we are afraid to embrace joy. We are so afraid of losing joy that we often do not allow ourselves to experience it in the moment. Again, the fear that we actually *can* create, that we actually *are* a part of the Creator, is there because we don't trust in ourselves to actually create what is in our highest good.

We are very confused about what joy is; we go around labeling what is not joy and what cannot bring us joy. We agree that money can't bring us joy, and we have come to realize that material things bring us only a momentary fleeting sensation of joy. But how do we tap into true joy?

In order to experience full joy that bubbles up from within us, we must remember our union with Source. In this space, we are so filled with love that it is pure bliss, and yet we are afraid to surrender into that to trust in it. Why? Because we fear that if we remember that Oneness, the bliss of being connected to All That Is, we will lose our individual self.

Joy is actually one of the emotions that is most closely tied to fear on a physical level. Think of the physiology of these emotions. To really bring it to mind, imagine yourself on a rollercoaster. The sensation in your stomach as you experience that thrill is a similar biological expression to that of joy: "having knots in your stomach" or "having butterflies." When we move beyond our comfort zone, it is often difficult to determine whether our body is reacting to joy or fear because they are so similar. How we choose to label that body sensation can often determine how we respond to it.

The primitive part of us will flare up when we begin to expand beyond our limited view of separation. There is an added part to this dance with joy. When we find a means, through meditation, prayer, or partnership, to tap into that pure bliss, it feels like ecstasy, and we want that. However, unless it is our time to cross, that bliss is usually followed by the harsh crash back into the illusion of separateness. One of the most painful experiences on the path to Oneness is feeling that crash back into the illusion after have had the bliss of experiencing Oneness with God. So until we learn to navigate as both the observer and the participant, we will actually sabotage our experience with joy in order to avoid the letdown when that emotion passes.

All emotions are fluid. As long as we are human, we have the full spectrum of emotions flowing through our experience. When we align with the love that flows in every moment, we will be able to experience the emotion of joy in its fullness in each moment. As we move deeper into the understanding of Oneness, the observer will remain in love and joy at all times, even as the participant experiences more difficult emotions of pain. The mere joy of having the ability to explore life with all of its various experiences will allow the observer in you to experience joy even in your most difficult moments. In this space, joy, like love, never ends.

≈ 14 ≈

The Human Emotion of Love

In the embrace of Enchanted One, I remember the eternal vibration of divine love. From this space, I am free to open my heart to love others unconditionally and without exception.

≈

We have already explored the core conflict that humans have with divine, unconditional love. The pull to surrender into Oneness is as strong as the pull to hold onto the separateness of the human experience, and that conflict is resolved as we align with spirit and open to embracing our emotions on Earth.

Love as an earthly emotion, however, is another exploration within itself. The human emotion of love is conditional. We are taught from a young age that love is to be earned. In fact, it is ingrained in our core belief that God is separate and we must earn God's love. And if we are not worthy of unconditional love from our Creator, if even God's love is fickle, then how can we possibly trust in the love of another human?

Our fear of losing ourselves in love (which is also our greatest desire) is so strong that, as humans, we have created many rules around the expression of this emotion. We interpret certain acts as expressions of love. We generally offer love to those we believe will return it—or at least not reject it. If someone rejects our expression of love, we are crushed and withdraw from them.

We have bought into so many rules around love in our human relationships that it is often difficult to remember what the emotion actually is. We feel ourselves opening and closing to the flow of love. We spend lifetimes trying to find love and partnership, and lifetimes sabotaging it. When we do feel an instance of love with another person, we cling to that feeling so much that we forget to allow its flow in the moment. We cling to moments of feeling love like we cling to photos of a friend who has died.

To surrender to another human being is an emotionally "dangerous" experience. I have always had an innate ability to see the reflection of God in others. No matter what another's behavior, I tend to see their perfect self. This is a gift, but when I was younger it caused a great deal of pain for me. I would embrace people, seeing only their higher self, and be hurt and devastated when their human self treated me in hurtful ways that conflicted with what I was seeing as pure love.

It is difficult to trust in the human expression of love because, in that reduced form, the emotion of love is conditional and based on the behaviors and choices of others. I came to a point where I would say, "I don't trust people, but I trust in my self and my connection to Creator, so I can open my heart to anyone." I learned to put my faith not in the human condition of love but in the endless flow of God's love. In that space, I embrace my relationships with other humans. And the more I connect to the endless flow of divine love, the more complete I feel and the more I am able to embrace the human experience. I find now that I am able to trust humans because the ebb and flow of human emotion no longer frightens me. I understand it. I embrace it, and I experience it for what it is.

Divine love remains constant, while human emotion is constantly changing. The more I understand this, the more I am able to consciously accept people with unconditional love for their personal process. When I allow myself to see both the higher self and the human expression of a person, I am able to understand where they are in their process and it no longer feels like a personal attack when they express conflicting emotions. In this space, I choose to love everyone who enters my life for the whole of who they are, both their beautiful soul and their evolving human expression.

≈ 15 ≈

Mastery of Emotions

Enchanted One ~ We gather together in remembrance now. Embracing our power of emotions as our gateway, we find peace within ourselves, and it is then reflected in our world. Standing with an open heart, loving without limitation, I reflect the Enchanted One to others through my love.

∾

In truth, the only way to truly experience love on Earth is to open our hearts to the love of the divine. To do this, we must be willing to keep our hearts open to *all* emotions. It is impossible to shut our heart to one emotion without shutting out the flow of love too. What I have come to understand is that, when we attempt to protect ourselves from difficult emotions, we disconnect from our Heart Center, or our emotional self. This is an instinct that most of us are not even aware of.

The moment there is a "threat" to our emotional well-being, we shut down to protect ourselves from the pain we are about to experience. Ironically, the pain actually comes from the act of shutting down, not the situations that trigger that response. As soon as we shut down, we feel the instant relief that comes from the sensation of being emotionless; however, what we have actually done is disconnect ourselves from the endless flow of divine love, the very energy that would support us in the emotional experience. In that moment of guarding our heart or "protecting" ourselves from the pain, we are falling into the illusion of separateness, and in this space we cannot feel the support of the love that is wrapping us in our fullness.

The key, then, is to keep our heart open at that exact moment before we are aware of closing it. If we do this we *will* experience the "threatening" emotion, but we will be so filled with the endless flow of love that the painful emotion will be fleeting and transformative. True pain is in the illusion of separateness, so when we stop that at the source, at the precise moment we are shifting into that illusion, we do not experience the depth of despair that comes from believing the illusion.

When Magdalene first made me aware of this, she told me she was no longer going to "allow me the luxury of shutting my heart down." At this point, I had already remembered my Oneness with All That Is. I had walked through a tremendous amount of grief and had allowed love to fill me at the most difficult moments. I had learned to live as the observer and the participant in each moment, and so I was surprised' to discover how many times my instinct was still to disconnect and how much less painful life was when I did not fall into that illusion of protecting myself from emotion.

Magdalene placed her hand on my heart at the instant I felt threatened and was preparing to disconnect.

It felt like a fire on my heart, and it was powerful enough to distract me from the emotional trigger I was experiencing in the moment. And as soon as I shifted my attention to the sensation of fire in my Heart Center, I felt wrapped in the endless flow of divine love. I remembered my Oneness with All That Is, and in that moment, when I turned my attention back to the situation that had triggered my fear, I no longer felt the power of its threat. I still felt the emotion of the moment—fear, anger, grief, whatever it was—but the sensation was wrapped in so much love that the emotion did not have power over me and moved through me like the flow of water over a rock in a stream. It simply *was*. I saw the situation with unconditional love. I experienced it and continued moving on my journey with clarity.

Magdalene offers this gift to you now. She offers you the gift of helping you to reconnect with your wholeness, with the unconditional love that is your birthright. We are never alone. Separation is illusion; the truth is that we are One in an endless flow of love. If you are ready to surrender to that flow, simply ask. Simply be willing to allow divine love to flow in you at every moment of your life. Intend to have this awareness, and watch it take form in your life.

A Message from Magdalene

I have spoken before of time not being linear, but stacked. Even the evolution that you are a part of—which is an illusion but is very real as you live in it—even that evolution is a part of the process of our understanding, a ring that will circle on itself. The end of time is the beginning of time, because this ring circles back. This is where we are now. The golden ring, the snake swallowing its tail of completion, is upon us. Will you wake up and notice completion? This is not an event that happens to you. It is an event that happens within you . . .

You are the universe . . . and you are a part of this union . . . I tell you this now so you will understand that the energies will increase more and more. Those of you with eyes open will experience periods of time like this when the energies will feel very intense, but each of you in your individual ways is getting more and more used to that . . . and your lifetimes themselves will settle. Do you see that as you do your individual work and you learn, you live in passion, and you embrace all of your emotions, all of them, the entire spectrum? You have the ability to be present and to be the observer at the same time. At each time, you have the ability to choose which one you will focus your attention on. At the same time, you have awareness of all. You have the ability to see your own individual struggles as something that you are walking through very clearly and profoundly, while at the same time you can see the smallness of these concerns in the whole picture of your ascension and the ascension of Mother Earth. As you see the option of both the bigger picture and the smaller picture in the time in which you are existing, you will feel completely harmonized with the ability to be present in each emotion.

Many of you, in your searching for awareness and understanding, have moved so far into the role of the expansive observer that you have detached yourselves from the emotions. Somewhere along the journey, many of you know that you have done this. You do have the ability to do this. That is why it is safe now as you move to this level; it is safe for you to feel passionate anger. Even as you feel passionate anger, you are the observer, so at any moment you have the ability to turn it, redirect it, or turn it off . . . so you do not have to fear that if you say, "I want to kill that person," you will really kill that person. When you realize this . . . I am not saying this as a joke . . . you will understand that it is safe now for you to have extreme pain, extreme anger, extreme fear, or jealousy. It is safe to allow these emotions to be present in the body because you are also the observer. At the same time that you let that stream of energy and consciousness move through your body, you also remain in the awareness that it is an illusion . . . that at any moment you can move yourself to a different level of the vibration, reconnecting with your Oneness with God. And it will dissipate immediately because it does not exist within the space of God's love. In that space, you only experience love. As you clear yourselves, and as you acknowledge this ability, at any moment you can choose what you will experience. That is what makes you the God Within.

Each one of you reading this now is learning this. You are mastering this in your own way. I apologize, but how do you master this if you do not experience extreme emotions of pain, anger, hurt, greed, grief, love, joy, celebration, and passion? All of these emotions . . . this is what Earth is about. This is why God created Earth, so that we could explore emotion. Somewhere along the way, people became so frightened of emotion. Emotions were so powerful that people began to categorize those that were "good" and those that were "bad." They split, and the ones who split the most were called schizophrenic . . . and yet all of you were split. Do you understand this? Do you understand that the only way to make yourself whole . . . the only difference between you and one whom you have given label to is your ability to discern, to be the observer? How quickly you can step into the role of observer when necessary! And now that you have learned how to be both the participant and the observer, it is time for the emotions to be brought to the surface so that you can feel. This is why I say that my treasure box has been opened, and everything in it: emotions.

As our hearts—our treasure chests—open, we release the emotions that we have hidden. As we release these as individuals and as a group, we open the space for love. It is impossible to suppress one emotion without suppressing them all, so when we say to ourselves, "Where has the love gone, the peace, and the joy?" look inside yourself. Connect with your God the Creator and together move into the depth of emotion, for it is there that you will feel the power of love.

When love becomes unconditional, when love becomes about service rather than need, it will move mountains. Literally. As this Earth ascends, the mountains are shaking, the oceans are screaming, the sky is roaring, because the vibration of love is increasing and the dense energies that are within our Mother Earth, that are within your soul, are shaking up, loosening so that they can vibrate once again in the true vibration of God's pure love . . .

—Magdalene, *as channeled through Sheila*

Living from Wholeness

When we have opened our hearts to embrace the full spectrum of emotions in our life, we begin to master the lessons that these emotions gift us. In this state, we are remembering our Oneness and our humanness at the same time. In this space, as we move forward with an open heart and mind aligned as one, we are embraced by the divine love of All That Is, and yet we still have human thoughts and limitations. We are still aware of the emotions of fear and doubt and uncertainty. We are as afraid of our weaknesses as we are of our power. And so, as we move forward to expand our understanding and to call in the possibility of instant manifestation in our lives, there arises a conflict inside of us: the ego, screaming, "No! Don't go to the light!"

Recall that the ego inside of us is the primitive self that has attached itself to our human experience so we can remain here on Earth. Recall the words of Isis when she told us that the Earth is a playground to explore emotions. Isis has said that in Creation, All That Is expanded Itself first to the Alpha and Omega of divine love and reflection, the male and the female polarities, in order to experience love in a deeper form outside of Itself—just as when we look at someone we love and feel overwhelmed by the beauty within them. Then that same beautiful light, All That Is, God's love, expanded further and created the full spectrum of emotions, still with the power of instant manifestation. In that space, we, as our part of All That Is, were beautiful, vibrant Gods and Goddesses, reflections of God and Goddess, the Alpha and Omega, in a form that allowed even more diversity and expansion, a form that allowed for the full spectrum of emotions.

All of us, in our lineage back to Oneness, were a part of that in some form, because we are all one. As that occurred, we had no understanding of emotion; it was our first experience with emotion. And so the spectrum of fear, anger, doubt, jealousy, grief, joy, bliss, and all of those emotions was ready to be explored. The power in that stage was so embraced that we experienced instant manifestation. However, we did not have the experience or understanding of emotions, and neither did we have the gift of time and space to slow the process of manifestation. Our thoughts and feelings became realities; our anger, our wishes, and our fears were all manifested instantly.

This is the chaos that has been written about in all of the ancient stories of the Gods and the Goddesses. These stories have been written by humans and so have been reduced even more in understanding. However, if we open our minds and imaginations, we can understand what it would be like to be in our full power, with the full power and ability to manifest in any moment and with no understanding of emotions. That chaos is still ingrained inside of us; however, we are also returning to that full power of creation and manifestation because the cycle is completing itself. Now we are awakening.

Together, we created the human experience with time and space, limitation and separateness. That sluggish energy that we have said was so thick and mucky and hard to walk through . . . that same energy that we have been frustrated with for so many years as we have tried to create things in our lives and have had delay after delay, walking through that smog of energy . . . that very same energy was the gift that we created as souls in order to give ourselves the freedom to experience the full spectrum of emotions—to dissect, to understand, and to live with them without instantly creating from that space. It was the gift we created as souls so that we had time to learn. We created the gift of time to understand, embrace, and transform emotion, to allow our emotions to create for us in slow process, giving us the feedback that we needed.

Now that we have explored these emotions and continue to explore them, we are becoming purer vessels. As we unite with our understanding of the Alpha and the Omega, as we realign ourselves with the Creator, we embrace again our fullness, the whole Alpha and Omega within us, uniting the head and the heart. We have explored the world of emotions, we have reconnected with the Oneness, and we have awoken from the illusion of karma and the need for time and space. Now here we are, ready once again to step into our power of wholeness, to step into that alignment with creation in which we have the ability to experience wholeness once again, to create instantaneously. We are supported by the universe now more than ever, because enough souls on Earth have awoken to draw the universe into support of this energy. All That Is is giving access again to creation beyond time and space, to instant manifestation, so that we can close the circle and create heaven on Earth now, in this moment.

As the forerunners, the pioneers, who have the work of exploring emotions, who are understanding the process and are tapping into new access to the creation energy on Earth that is here for us now, we are being gifted the ability to create the lives we desire right now . . . and that scares the hell out of us! It scares the hell out of even those of us who have explored the world of emotions, who have opened to our remembrance of being One with God and lived in the vibration of God's love on Earth. Why? Because we remember that time in chaos. As we are all one, the part of us that remembers is afraid to embrace our power once again. And so we call the power to us and then we push it away; we call the love to us and then we push it away. We call the desire to us, the knowing to us, and then we push it away. We call Creation to us and then we push it away.

Let's step out of that now, because now we are being embraced in a new way. We are being embraced by the understanding that it all happens at once, and so we are all One. We are being embraced by the understanding that time is an illusion but also a tool that we can draw on whenever we desire. We are being embraced by the understanding that even the creation of our fears will not harm us because in the same instant we will create perfection, which will realign the fear that we create.

We do not have to be afraid of misusing this power of creation anymore, because we now have access within our own being, not only because of the work we have done as individuals but also because of the work that individuals have done to support the universe. What one soul does, every soul receives. And so we are embraced by those who are with us and those who have gone before us, and we embrace others in the knowing of this perfection. Now, at this time, as we are opening the star gate for the union of heaven and Earth, spirit and humans are beginning to integrate once again. There is no separation. We release our need for time and space. We can create whatever we desire. The only limits are the limits that we place upon creation. The only limits are the limits we place upon ourselves. Love never ends, and love is All That Is.

16

Isis: Questions and Answers
on the Subject of Emotions

This section consists of Isis's responses to questions addressed to her in the course of a channeling on emotions that was done for a group audience. Isis's words are italicized.

≈

I ask you now if you have questions for me about that which I have shown you today. It is so beautiful and so simple, and yet I know this is what we struggle most with in human form. I say to you that in spirit form, that pull to the touch of the heart, to the emotion, to the depth of God, that is Earth, that is emotion, it is so strong. It is all God. Ask me now that which will assist you in this remembrance.

Question: I'm working on having my emotions flow and not holding back and letting things go . . . is there anything else that can assist me in this process?

I smile at you because I remember this phase. This is why each of you shut down in the human world, because this re-shut the doors, re-shut the doors. Because when you open the floods of all those emotions, they do not go away. Do not think that if you have avoided emotion it goes away. When you suppress, when you push inward, it remains in your cellular body, and as soon as you are ready to do the work, it comes up like the Nile being filled. It is so full and so strong. It feels like you will not be okay.

Some people come with what you now medicate for, the depression . . . all of those feelings seem to overwhelm them. We say to you, you can ask for them to come in ways that you can tolerate, but there is a sense of purging when you open up, when you agree to open the heart again, to experience being in tune with what is happening, to realign your emotions with your journey. Before you can get to that place, you must release all of those emotions that you have suppressed. You may go through a period where you cry at the slightest thing. You may go through a period where you cry at a television commercial, or when you see a little girl across the street touch her daddy's hand. You may cry at the slightest thing. You may also get angry, if that is an emotion that you have suppressed.

Of course you need to do it in a healthy way that is not going to hurt anyone. You may feel yourself being very angry, and you may not want to be an angry person, but I say to you that feeling the anger is a way not to be an angry person. Suppressing anger is what will make you an angry person. It will leak out like steam from a teapot. It will just come out of you. You try so hard to control, but what you do is set up the most uncontrolled situation, and when you decide to align you actually get back into control, from the higher self. In the meantime, these extreme emotions from your lifetime—maybe many lifetimes—begin to purge, and we say to you, hang in there. It is not the rest of your life; it is very short-term. It moves very quickly. Anything you use, any energetic healing, the Reiki, the transmuting violet flame, the willingness to release things during dream state, the asking to work twenty-four hours a day . . . with anything you use, you can ask for assistance. A lot of this gets done during the dream state, with the willingness to feel it when it comes up. And some of it has to occur in the wake state, in the emotional field. However, you can use tools.

You can ask for assistance in purging what needs to be purged so that you can more quickly get into alignment. In that place, once this is purged and you remain open, you will feel love, you will feel fear, you will feel anger, you will feel. But love will always return, for that is the state of Truth, and all the other emotions as you get triggered will be very, very quick. You will feel them very deeply, but you will be in tune with what you need to do. You will know their message very quickly. You will know what you have to do to respond to them. You will very quickly, almost effortlessly, return to your state of love, but you will do that while experiencing emotions.

And we say to you about your willingness to open to those emotions: let those floodgates move. They will very quickly get you there when you are in that space. If you begin to shut back down, you will prolong the process. And if you shut spirit out and don't use the tools that they have to help you, if you do it all on the emotional and mental plane, it will slow down the process. Either way, whether you do it just on the physical and emotional plane, in the slower way, or whether you let spirit in, it will result in the end place of being purged, of getting your emotions in line. If you shut the gates back—which is what you've been doing, what the human race has been doing for so long—if you shut the gates back, it will keep building up and up. This is what we are attempting to shift now.

Question: What about when emotions come up and the person is not physically there?

It does not matter if the person is not physically there, because you are not responsible for that person's emotions. The person is merely a reflection to you, so you can do the work within you. Really, it is completely irrelevant whether that person is near you or far away, or engaging in this journey or not. The emotions, the willingness to feel the emotions, to experience the emotions, to allow yourself to move through them, to understand them and to let them release as you make the journey . . . if the emotions are there, allow yourself to experience them. They're there because you have to do something different, because you have to claim something different, because you have to choose something different. You chose that, but it really has nothing to do with the other person.

There are times when two of you will engage each other and talk out to the deepest level . . . the mirror will go to a deep level of continuing to sustain itself in a unity, either in deep love or in anger or in fear or in any of that where two or more people are participating in a journey. But even in those moments, you are only responsible for yourself. You act as a mirror to the other, and your awareness of the other person is only there for you to turn and look inward to what parts you need to focus on yourself.

You cannot say, "Well, I would be doing this work but the people around me won't," because it isn't their responsibility. They are merely your mirrors. The energies that flow between you are there to evoke emotions. It is your responsibility to follow the journey of each of those emotions to its final point of love. That might take a lifetime for some emotions, or it might take a minute, but it is your responsibility, not the other's. And you act as the mirror for the other person, and they will either choose to learn from that or not, and depending on how you reflect for each other, you will choose to journey together or not in the physical world.

Question: Isis, this sounds like it is easy to do in a meditation, but to do it in our lifetime here seems not that easy.

I do know what you are saying. I have experienced it. I know that in the vibration of Earth it is not easy to do. And I also know that the vibration of Earth is at a very difficult point, and you are the ones, you are the souls of greatness—or you would not be here. You look around at the world and you see the destruction, and you see all of the chaos, and you long for love. And you know that it is so difficult to hold this vibration on Earth, and the vibration that She exists in now, and yet you continue to journey, and you continue to seek love.

We have so much honor for you because you have come at one of the most difficult times in evolution; it is in the transition time back from the dark to the light. We say to you that you are honored for all attempts that you make here. What we would like most to give you, what I would like most to remind you of, is that you cannot destroy anything. God is All That Is, and God cannot be created or destroyed. Everything you see around you . . . Mother Earth, the animals, the people . . . nothing that is of God can be destroyed, and everything is of God.

So do not fear. One of the reasons you are so controlling . . . all of us humans . . . is that, when we began this journey, we thought we were so powerful that we would destroy with our emotions. And yet I say to you that nothing is so powerful that it can destroy God . . . and everything is God. The evolution is occurring as it is intended. The density that humans and the Earth are experiencing—the low vibration—is not punishment, is not a mistake. It is simply that, in that low vibration, we can recreate, we can explore those emotions that we feared so much because they will not have as great of an impact. Yet, at the same time, our love does not have as profound of an impact on the instantaneous level because the vibration is lower here on Earth.

But it is having an impact. All of the journey has an impact, and what it impacts is the ability to understand, to expand, to remember that all of these expressions, once moved to the truest form, are expressions of love. There is nothing else. When you allow yourself to journey in each one of them, it is having a profound effect on the evolution, even if you do not feel it in your instant lives. So it is with much gratitude that we tell you: we understand.

—Isis, as channeled through Sheila

17

A Call From Isis

As I come forward here tonight, I penetrate each one of you and I place my hands upon you. But I do not place my hand upon you with that soothing comfort that my beloved sister Mary and her partner Yesu often place upon you. Today I wish to infuse you with passion; I wish to infuse you with an energy source that is so strong; I wish for you to feel now the penetrating eclectic fire of God the Creator, for you are a part of this, for you are the fire of passion of the Gods.

So you speak here tonight about fire, and I am saying to you: embrace it, let it burn, let it burn across the Earth. So many movies coming out now about the Earth burning up, but I say to you this is not an Earth fire. Let it be the fire of passion; let it move forward now. Let us join in the movement. Let us step beyond our limitations. Let us forget that we are in the illusion of separateness and let us drop now those lists . . .

Put into the fire the lists of all the reasons why now is not a good time; why now is not the time to embrace; why now is not the time to step into your power; why now is not the time to become abundant in finances; why now is not the time to live with your passion; why now is not the time for romance; why now is not the time for a child. Whatever it is that you are resisting, write it on the paper in your mind and throw it into the fire now. For as many reasons as there are for why *not*, there will be as many reasons for *why*. So I ask you now to take a paper in your mind's eye and write both lists: "*Why* should I move forward; *why* should I create the life I desire?" and, "*Why* shouldn't I?" . . . why now is correct . . . and why now is wrong. Write them in your mind now . . . the dos and the don'ts, the shoulds and the should nots, the pros and the cons. Because as long as you sit in that battle, you will stay there forever. You will stay there forever. When you simply drop both, when you simply drop both into the fire within your mind's eye, you will watch that fire turn to purple, to violet, to the transmuting violet flame. Then, in your mind's eye it will form deeper, into pinks and greens, rose, blue, indigo, yellow, and orange.

In your mind's eye, look at that fire, the vibrant colors dancing so high above you . . . three times your height, everywhere you turn. It is creeping towards you. Stand still, mesmerized by its beauty. Allow the fear to come up. Feel it in your body, acknowledge and recognize . . . if your thoughts start to run, there is nowhere to run. It is all around you, simply coming towards you from every direction, and yet it is beautiful. It is warm. It is hot, and it is crackling. Be aware of your body, be aware of your thoughts as you imagine this fire coming towards you. Acknowledge your thoughts, don't try to control them. Let all of your thoughts come to the surface. Scan your body and see which part of you is in reaction.

In your mind's eye, the fire moves in; every part of you is now on fire. You are on fire in the flame of fearlessness, the same flame of fear . . . it is all one, for where there is fear there is passion, where there is love there is fear. Nothing is separate. Don't think about where you are going or where you have come from. Don't think about what is right or wrong. Don't figure it out. Simply allow the fire to burn through every layer of you, let it burn the thoughts, the emotions, the body sensations. Let it burn everything that comes up. If you want to resist it, acknowledge that, but allow it to continue to burn through you. This is passion. This is what it is to be truly alive. To be truly alive is to feel and to know at the same time that you are the Creator.

Why are you afraid to create the life that you desire? Because you still believe that you are separate. You still believe that you can mess up. You still believe that you were abandoned by your Creator. You still believe on some level of your cellular body that this life is a punishment. Let that belief burn away now, let the core burn away now . . . because at the core is the illusion that you were abandoned by your Creator . . . that you are separate from the power of All That Is . . . because there is only truly fear in separateness . . . and yet it transforms to passion in the Oneness. It has been here to keep you safe, to lead you back. It was here to guide you until you remembered that you were never separate, and all the fear that you have come to know, all the things that you have identified as threats in your life, all the things that you have convinced yourself are frightening, are covering up the core belief that you are separate. The knowledge that you are powerful is so frightening that you have embraced the fear of separateness.

Bring to the surface now the very belief that you may be God, that you may be capable of having the life that you desire, that you may know everything inside of yourself, and that you may have the power to guide others forward to that remembrance. What does that mean? If you are possibly that powerful, is the fear coming up that you have failed? For if you are that powerful, why have you waited so long? I challenge you with these thoughts because I know that they are inside of you. If you are so powerful, why is the world so filled with fear and hate? If God is in every one of us, what are we creating? If you are still human enough to feel the emotions of fear, anger, pain, and jealousy, and perhaps even hate in a moment, what if you created from that space? What have you created? I say to you: I was there at the beginning of time, when we were whole, when we remembered our wholeness, the Alpha and the Omega.

This comes back to the core. This is why everyone on the Earth is experiencing this, and this is why the waves are coming through so strong, and I press you here today, because there is only one fear. It comes from the beginning of time. It is embedded in each one of you. If you do not acknowledge this you will live in the illusion and you will dance around, and you will create other fears. For the fears come innately through you because each one of you as self is attached to the Oneness . . .

When the Oneness expanded Itself in order to embrace and to feel and to acknowledge love, It moved into the Alpha and the Omega, where It could see the reflection of Itself. In this space, Creator could deepen Its love. Then the Alpha and Omega expanded further to the individual beings that are many more than us here on Earth. It is more. It is those beings that are known in mythology from all of the directions as Gods and Goddesses. What are the stories that have been passed down since that time? They are filled with fighting and pain.

How many have heard of the Gods fighting in mythology? How many have heard of the duality that occurred? How many stories are there of the destruction that the Gods created in one single passionate emotion? Why are so many of you afraid of that in your core? Because you know in your vibration that that is a phase of creation.

In your core, you know that there was a phase in which the Oneness expanded Itself so that It could feel the whole spectrum of emotions. In that phase before Earth was created, there was instant manifestation . . . things were being created and destroyed in an instant, with all of the beings that were alive at that point. Everyone on Earth is a lineage of that because we are all one, and so it is in your vibration as it is in everyone's. In that phase, it was chaos because suddenly, with great power, there were these emotions that had never been felt, never been explored, and things were bouncing all over the place. In your core, you believe that you are being punished in this illusion of separateness because of that time, because you believe that, when you were connected to that vibration that was so powerful, you wronged, you made a mistake, and therefore to reach that power again would be to destroy, would be chaos.

I say to you now: It is not the beginning, it is the end. We are completing this cycle, and the power that you hold within you now to move to that level, to remember your Oneness with God, to remember your ability to create, to be an instant vibration of manifestation, is now embraced, yes, with the whole experiment of time. You went through the process of the illusion, of separateness, so that you could explore emotions. All of those times that you were on the wheel of karma, believing that illusion . . . all those times were of benefit because you now are capable, you have embraced emotion enough now that you can *wake* up, you can remember it, you can understand it.

When you step back into your power, you will still experience emotion and you will be able to manifest instantly, but it will not carry the same sensation of being out of control because you will not attach to the emotions. You understand them; you have mastered them. You will delay manifesting when you need to, you are of substance now. You have done the work and so there is nothing to fear . . . I know that each one of you began this chapter thinking that you would attack your little fears . . . they are so tiny because they are just masking the core fear. And the core fear is that you *are* powerful and that you are *not* separate from God . . . because if you remember that, then you know you can create the life you desire. And if there is any part inside of you that feels like you were wrong in that vibration when you were first created, when your vibration was connected to that creation, it will flare up and say, "Wait! We are not ready . . . "

So this flame of passion, of fear, of fearlessness, embraces you now, and you hold the space for so many others as we allow that to move through you, into the cells beyond your thought patterns, to release your core fear, taking with it the power of the illusional fears that you have been dancing with. They will no longer have power over you because you will have faced the core fear . . .

I ask you now to sit in a meditative state and allow that flame to burn through you. When you feel that it has burned to the core of your fears, allow it to expand outward into the world, gifting it to all those who are ready to remember.

I thank you and I honor you and I call you back to your place of power . . . I challenge you now to create the life you desire, for there are no limits before you . . . I know that you have the ability right now, in this moment, to create the world you desire, and that this thought creates fear . . . I know that your thoughts may be rising up with all the reasons why you can't, why the power is in someone else's hands, and I say let those fears burn away . . . do not fight them. Do not resist these thoughts.

—*Isis, as channeled through Sheila*

Postscript

Cherry Blossom Love

Life is beautiful. I am happy. I choose love always. I do not wish to live in the past or the future, only in the moment that is before me in each instant. I choose cherry blossom love in every moment: In each second, I choose to let go of my fears of the future and the scars of my past and embrace the flow that is offered to me with each single breath . . . and then the next . . . and then the next, always releasing, always allowing the love to be new and fresh, always allowing the person I am loving to grow, to redefine him or herself, to become more of who she or he is.

To do this, I must be willing to let go of the past, to release my scars, and to take responsibility for them, to remember that any person who I believe abandoned me or wronged me with his actions was not trying to hurt me. He or she was simply trying to find his or her own truth in that moment . . . just like me, that person is growing and exploring and learning to love unconditionally with each breath . . . and if I choose to hold him or her to the past, then I am choosing not to love them, not allowing them to be who they are in each moment, not remembering that everything in my path is perfect, that everything my lover has done, whether it caused pain or joy, has been an expression of his love for me and his search for truth within himself. Love never ends . . . not even with death.

I am the only one who has ever caused a scar or a wound on my body, my soul, or my emotions. No one else has the power to do that. My actions put me in the place, the situation, the emotional confusion that allowed the pain to occur. I am responsible, and only I can choose to be scarred. Only I can choose to be healed, and only I am hurt by the scars I form in my mind.

As I open to love, I am faced with the memories of what hurt me in the past. I didn't run from them . . . I cried, I yelled, I expressed, I moved on, and so now in each situation I am being given a chance to start over. Everything that occurred was perfect; it allowed me to grow, to become more of who I am. So I have a choice now to believe that everything was perfect for my soul to grow in love, and I chose that all along. It did not stop me from being angry; it did not hold the grief at bay. It did not make the emotions go away, but it did allow me to heal . . .

Even so, I have seen through the years more than once when I have felt those old fears . . . a person will respond to me in a certain way and I will feel my whole body react as if the past will repeat itself. And yet each time I feel that, I look at it, I get through it and I learn from it, and I learn more about myself . . . I sort out between what is my past, my reaction, and I let that go. I look at the *moment*. And each time I do, it is never as bad as the past. And each time I do, I trust myself more. And the more I trust myself, and the more I trust love itself, the safer I am to open my heart to love, even with those I have been hurt by. When I do this, I set us *both free* . . .

the ones who have hurt me are free to grow, free to be the more loving people they are trying to be, and I am free to be loved.

I trust in myself. I trust in myself to create love and happiness in my life. I trust in myself to live in joy with or without partnership in my life. I trust in myself to choose the form of partnership that is correct for me in each second. I trust in myself to protect my children, not from love or pain, but to teach them that they are okay no matter what and that it is okay and safe to love when you are whole and full within yourself.

I choose cherry blossom love . . . to love a lifetime in an instant . . . no past, no future, just the present. That is the only way to fully love. I trust myself . . . my ability to live with joy and love no matter where life takes me. And in that trust, I can open my heart to love each person fully in each moment . . . trusting my heart . . . my gut . . . my intuition to lead me down a perfect and beautiful path.

Appendix: Prayers and Meditations

Prayers for Self-Awakening

I do not put my feet on the ground in the morning without saying a prayer of surrender. I surrender my day and everything in it. If there is something in my day that I am concerned about, I take the time to specifically ask spirit to assist me in that area. Then—and this is the key—*I trust* that it is done. I trust every decision I make during the day, even if it feels like I made the "wrong turn" on my way to the grocery store. I trust there is a reason. I surrender to that knowing and allow myself to *be* in the moment. If the day seems to be a struggle and one thing after another seems to be hard, then I stop and check in with myself. I re-center myself and say a prayer of surrender again, not because my Creator and guides have abandoned me but because I have abandoned them. I do that more than I would like to admit.

Have you ever asked God for help on something and then, after waiting for what feels like forever, you decide you'd better take some action and solve it on your own? "Here, God, take this from me. I don't know what to do and I know that You will guide me. I trust You to lead me and make this unfold in perfection. God? Hellooooo! Is this mic on? Did you forget? Maybe I'd better handle this one . . . not sure You quite get it. I think You are misunderstanding the severity of this situation . . . "

Sometimes we surrender, but when it is not taken care of in *our* time, or in the way we planned, we take it back. And then we wonder why things are so tangled. When things feel off balance, check in with yourself. Ask, "Did I just take this back? Am I trusting in the universe to align for my highest good?" If not, find your way back to your center with prayer, meditation, exercise, or whatever brings you back to your center of peace. Each time you will remember to return to that place more often, and eventually you will remain in the center of peace—even in the most turbulent and emotional times of your life.

~

Dear God/Goddess/Creator of All That Is, all the beings of light, ascended masters, and spirit guides who are with us today, we give thanks for your presence. I surrender this day to you. I ask that you make me a pure and open vessel of your love and your teaching. Take complete control of my spiritual, emotional, and physical bodies. All That Is, guide me to see love in every situation I face today. I ask that everything that flows through me today be in accordance with your divine plan, and that each person in my life today receive everything they need on their own path of light. I ask my guides to take us each to the next level of our development, and I give thanks for all of the gifts that pass through me. Amen.

Dear God/Goddess/Creator of All That Is, today I choose to let go of everything in my life that keeps me from living my full potential and serving my Creator in the highest. I walk through the pain of grief, knowing and welcoming the space that will follow. I call to that space of emptiness love in all of its forms, that I may draw to me the perfect vibration for my continued healing and service to Mother Earth and all who dwell within Her vibration. I release all of my illusions of form that keep me from experiencing the joy of the miracle of life and love. I give thanks for the grace of divine love that surrounds me, and I welcome it to penetrate every cell of all my bodies, that I may love deeply and with joy.

Meditation to the God/Goddess/Self

It is recommended that you record this meditation in order to experience its full benefit. Similar meditations are available on CD for purchase at *sheilapplegate.com*.

As you sit there, very relaxed and comfortable, I ask that you take a deep breath in . . . and release. Breathe in love . . . and release fear. Breathe in hope . . . and release doubt. Continue to breathe deeply and rhythmically as you feel your mind and body becoming more and more relaxed. All distracting thoughts float away like puffy white clouds in the bright blue sky. They have no power over you.

As you sit there, very relaxed and comfortable, you begin to feel, sense, or see beneath your feet a beautiful disc of white light. Into this white light will come three colors. The first color is for your physical healing and balancing. Allow this to enter into the white light, circling around and around. The next color is for your emotional healing and balancing. Allow that to enter into the white light, circling around and around. The third color is for your spiritual healing and balancing. Allow that to enter into the white light, circling around and around, until the light returns to white with the vibration of all three colors within it.

Now you begin to feel, sense, or see the beautiful tingling vibration as the white light enters the soles of your feet, healing, blending, and cleansing your physical, emotional, and spiritual bodies. The light continues up through your calves and into your knees. Take a moment now to feel the difference in vibration above and below your knees, and then allow the light to continue upward once again, through your thighs and into your hips. The light enters your base chakra, circling around and around and cleansing now all of the emotions of fear, anger, guilt, and doubt. Those emotions that you felt were unworthy of expression and pushed downward are now cleansed and purified in the light.

Allow the light to continue upward once again into your second chakra, bringing your vibration into balance and purity. Now the light continues into your solar plexus just below your ribcage, the emotional center of your body, bringing all of your emotions into balance. Allow the light to continue upward into your lungs, that you may breathe in divine love, into your heart and your heart chakra, that you may feel only divine love. Allow the light to continue upward to your shoulders, where you release now the burdens that you have carried for other people. You took them in love, but now you know better. They are not yours to carry. Release them into the light, that they may return to their rightful owners with love, so that the lessons may be learned.

Allow the light to move down your arms and into your hands, that all those you touch will feel the divine power of healing in your love. Allow the light to move upward once again into your throat and your throat chakra, that you may speak only the truth . . . into your ears, that you may hear only the truth . . . into your eyes and your third eye, that you may see only the truth. The light continues upward through your crown chakra, the top of your head, where it pours back down over you like a beautiful water fountain, until you are completely filled and surrounded by the beautiful white light of protection. Nothing shall enter this space that is not for your highest good.

In this beautiful pillar of white light, you are now completely protected and balanced. I ask that you draw your attention now to your feet, where you see rising upward the beautiful transmuting violet flame. This flame will transmute for you now all negative thoughts, feelings, desires, and memories, returning them to the perfection of white light and divine love. Allow the violet flame to move through you.

Now draw your attention back to your heart chakra, where you see the beautiful threefold flame of pink, yellow-gold, and blue, male, God and female vibrations. As you focus your energy on the flame within your heart, it begins to expand, bringing you into complete balance with your male, female, and God vibrations within you. I ask that you draw your attention back to the top of your head, the crown chakra, where you see, feel, or sense a beautiful cord of white light. Follow this cord upward until you come to your higher self. Welcome your higher self downward, blending with your physical, emotional, and spiritual bodies.

Focusing back on the cord, you follow it upward until you come to your I Am presence, your individual piece of God vibration, a white causal body with rings of color all around you. Allow your I Am presence to move downward, filling your higher self, your spiritual self, your emotional self, and your physical self. You are completely aligned and connected with the Creator.

Now I ask that you draw your attention once again to your Heart Center, where you see a beautiful beam of white light coming from your heart, forming a crystal star in the center of the room. We place into this crystal star now our *intention of all those we wish to receive healing today. Into this crystal star we now place Mother Earth and all who dwell within her, that She may feel the healing vibration of our love to aid in Her ascension. We give thanks to all the beings of light who carry our healing intentions outward today.*

I ask that you draw the beam back into the center of your heart, where you, too, receive a healing . . . where, as you give, so shall you receive. Now draw your attention back to the beautiful pillar of white light that is all around you, and in this space you become once again aware of your own physical body, of this room, of this time, and of this space. And when you are ready, take a deep breath and open your eyes.

About the Author

 As a clinical therapist, motivational presenter, author and teacher, Sheila Applegate's passion is to provide a forum for people to process emotion and integrate spiritual understanding into their daily lives.

Sheila earned a Bachelor's Degree of Social Work from Syracuse University, and a Master's Degree in Clinical Social Work from the University of Maryland. In 1998, after years of studying metaphysics, Sheila was ordained as minister through the Light of Divine Truth Foundation.

For over 20 years, Sheila has combined her broad formal training with her continual personal awakening to bring forth the message of Oneness through Divine Love. As a messenger of Spirit, she embraces and connects with the vibration of the Divine Feminine. Sheila encourages people to embrace their passions as service on earth by living within the Spirit of Enchanted Oneness. Visit Sheila at *www.sheilapplegate.com*